EXPLOSION ON EVERGREEN AVENUE

Ken Lord

KenMar Publications
Syracuse, NY
2020

Copyright © 2020 by Ken Lord

All rights reserved. This book or any portion thereof may not be reproduced or used without the express written permission of the publisher except for brief quotations in a book review or scholarly journal.

First printing: 2020

ISBN: 978-1-716-43070-1

Ken Mar Publications
Syracuse, New York

Table of Contents

Cast of Characters

There are many characters in this story. The important ones are:

Parents of Charles:
    Father: William Virgil Bennett
    Mother: Mary Bowman

Parents of Denise:
    Father: James Butler Bennett (died 1981)
    Mother: Callie May McGlone (died 1990)

Three brothers of Denise:
    David—murdered 1972
    Louis—wife Joyce, daughter Jill
    Fred—girlfriend Maude/Wife Waynetta

Charles Butler Bennett (husband/father)
Denise Bennett (wife/mother)
    Child—Jocelyn Barbara Bennett (Jocey) (1950)
    Child—Scott Allen Bennett (Scotty) (1952)
    Child—Donald Hefka Bennett (Donny) (1953)
    Child—Catherine Jean Bennett (Cathy) (1954)
    Child—Shirley Louise Bennett (1955- 1981)
    Child—Jason Paul Bennett (1958)

Danny Golden (affair/father)
Denise Bennett (mother)
    Child—Liza Mary Bennett (1961)

Rayford Mickey Dawson (Lappan?) (Affair/father)
Denise Bennett (mother)
    Child—Elizabeth Ann Bennett (Lizard Ann) (1965)

Sam the Beagle
Henry the Beagle
Greta the Doberman

Denise's girlfriend and confidant: Patti (important to the story).

You may wish to refer to this list periodically.

Foreword

This is a story about a woman named Denise Bennett, who suffered from Post-Traumatic Stress Disorder (PTSD). The story is not as a clinician might describe it but is as a homemaker and mother of eight experienced it. This is not an authoritative work on PTSD.

The story began on Christmas Eve, 1958 with the death of Denise's husband, Charles, but it haunted her for the remainder of her life. Denise died, I believe, sometime following 2015, in Tucson, Arizona. A check of the records I could find did not produce the name of the person I knew at that time.

For the record, "Denise" was not her real name, nor was it even the name under which she traveled for the balance of her life. In fact, the only real name in this book is that of the author. If some names happen to align with real persons, this is coincidental. These names were provided by Mrs. Bennett in the twilight of her life. The reasons for this will be detailed in the book and are the result of a self-imposed witness protection program.

I first met Denise Bennett (not the name she was using) at a yard sale in Tucson, Arizona, in 2005. I had been hospitalized and it was determined that I should not continue my business. Therefore, I had begun to write and generally stopped at yard sales to see if I could obtain inexpensive supplies. When I happened to mention that fact to the person holding the sale, I was overheard by Mrs. Bennett, a woman in her mid-seventies at that time, who said, "You're just the person I need."

Thus began a writing saga that would stretch the next four years, become interrupted when she dropped out of sight, and abandoned when I was widowed and left the state. It's now 2020. It's time to finish the story.

As a nation, we encountered PTSD during both world wars. During World War I, the condition was called *Shell Shock*. The Second World War labeled it as *Battle Fatigue*. It was not until the Vietnam War that the description of PTSD came into vogue and a part of the lexicon. Psychologists and psychiatrists have come to regard it as a potential outcome of any traumatic event in a person's life, and not merely one of the outcomes of armed conflict.

According to the Mayo Clinic, PTSD typically begins within three months of a traumatic event. This story will tell of recurring symptoms that began almost immediately and spanned seven decades. Despite any thoughts to the contrary, the condition never goes away. One merely learns to cope. Post-traumatic stress disorder symptoms, according to Mayo Clinic, may include:

- *Flashbacks or reliving the traumatic event for minutes or even days at a time.* Denise experienced this from the time of the accident.

- *Shame or guilt.* She still felt the guilt about having insisted on buying the house where the accident occurred. She told about the one severe argument she and her husband had that had been brought on by interference from her mother.

- *Upsetting dreams about the traumatic event.* Denise continued those dreams for more than sixty years.

- *Distress at anniversaries of the trauma.* She experienced those annually from the date of the event. Christmas is, obviously, the worst.

- *Efforts to avoid thoughts, feelings, and activities associated with the trauma.* She mastered the effort to avoid them all. She tried to avoid thinking or talking about the traumatic event. Unburdening herself to do this was not easy.

- *Feelings of detachment or estrangement from others and an inability to have loving feelings.* This dogged Denise for the entire time. Naturally, she had such feelings toward her children. For others, however, it does not exist.

- *Markedly diminished interest or participation in activities that once were an important source of satisfaction.* There were two reasons for this in Denise's life: she was busy working and caring for the kids and school. Otherwise, she lost interest.

- *Hyper vigilant.* Denise was very sensitive to noise. She told of working in a hospital with a large autoclave that made noise and produced steam, which constantly reminded her of steam radiators, the meaning of which will be evident in the first chapter.

- *Physical and psychological hypersensitivity*—not present before the trauma—with at least two of the following reactions: trouble sleeping (yes), anger (yes), difficulty concentrating (yes), exaggerated startle responses (yes), and physiological reactions to situations that remind you of the traumatic event (yes; she often cried).

- *Feeling emotionally numb, poor relationships, self-destructive behavior, trouble sleeping, memory problems.* Denise experienced them all. She carried self-destructive behavior to its nadir. To these low points in her life, she, in reaction, took extreme personal risks, and as a result lost much.

- *Post-traumatic stress disorder symptoms can come and go.* There may be more symptoms during times of higher stress or when symbolic reminders are experienced. The person with PTSD may relive the traumatic event numerous times; have upsetting memories or see reminders wherever she goes.

These physiological reactions may include an increase in blood pressure, a rapid heart rate, rapid breathing, muscle tension, nausea, and diarrhea. Denise experienced several of these.

One might ask why perhaps Denise didn't seek help for this condition. She did, unsuccessfully. She also had enough of a medical background to recognize that the "get over it" messages she received were insufficient support. Of the visits she had with counselors, none presented the coping strategies she developed for herself. Once she recognized that she never would—yea, never *could* get over it, she faced a choice: she could live as she had for more nearly three quarters of a century—or find a way to wrestle with her demons.

When Denise and I met, she learned that I write and I learned that she had a story worth telling. That which is documented here is the truth, as she saw it and expressed it to me, though we've changed names to protect both the guilty and the tender feelings of some who may still be alive. The name she has adopted for herself is a pseudonym. My name is accurate.

This has not been an easy book to put together. The lyric of a country song is most apropos: "I'm pickin' up bones, I'm pickin' up bones; exhumin' things that's better left alone. I'm ressurectin' memories…" You get the idea. This has not been merely a trip down memory lane for Denise. This has been, in some cases, sheer agony, for every memory exhumed has caused several more to surface, and not merely in a nice, neat, chronological sequence.

A memoir of this type should be presented in first person, and for the most part, it is. Writer's comments set the scenes and are included for edification where the facts or dialogs don't easily explain.

Ken Lord

Introduction

<u>Detroit, Michigan—Christmas Day, 1958</u>

He was killed instantly. I was sure of it. There was nothing I could do to help him. The children, wrapped in the maelstrom of this calamity, were now my priority.

We had rolled out extra early this morning. The plan had been in place for days—a late night trip to Grandma's, snug in bed in time for Santa Claus to arrive and do his thing, and then... and then. "Visions of sugar plums" was an apt description of what went on in the minds of the first five of our six children.

We get up early every morning, but today was Christmas. Their father and I felt the excitement of six rambunctious children, as one by one, pajama-clad legs and slipper-covered feet hit the floor in a rush to see if Santa Claus had arrived at midnight. The noise level rose to a roar when a peek out the front door onto the enclosed porch that held the tiny Spruce tree revealed that the pudgy little man had made it again this year.

The night before, his arrival had been in doubt. Dinner at Grandma's house had dragged on as we sought holiday fellowship—and a holiday drink or two—with infrequently seen siblings. The fellowship was palpable but lurking in Charles' and my minds were the twin problems of an oncoming snowstorm and the evaporating envelope of time necessary to extract hidden boxes and bags and get them wrapped and labeled before even the adults collapsed.

Between the last piece of pumpkin pie and the decision to leave, several of us had one—or perhaps two—too many mulled ciders. Or was it a hot toddy? I don't remember much, though I do recall an empty *Dewar's*—or was it a *Cutty Sark*—bottle in the trash. We'd had enough for my mother to demand that we each drink a strong cup of coffee "before you take those precious children home." I was sitting, drinking my coffee, when Charles came tramping in the back door, shaking the snow from his boots.

"There's more than a foot out there," he advised, "and it's comin' down heavy. We'd better be getting on."

Mother said, "Do you have chains, Charles?"

"Yes, Mother, we have chains. Detroit in the winter calls for chains, studs, or snow tires. Would you believe that we have all three?"

***

One by one, I roused the kids from the various places where they had fallen asleep. Jocey, old enough to dress herself, quickly put her snowsuit on. I stuffed the next three—Scotty, Donny, and Cathy—into their snowsuits, pulled up their hoods, and attached their mittens. The ones who were dressed sat on chairs by the door while Charles wrestled with their footwear.

While he did that, I bundled Shirley, three, and Jason (the baby)—now only ten months—into snowsuits and wrapped them snugly in a cotton cocoon, leaving nose and mouth exposed enough to breathe. I kissed Mother goodbye, wished everyone a Merry Christmas, kissed my brothers and sisters, and shook hands with the various in-laws.

Charles moved the kids, from oldest to youngest, out the door, through the snow, and into the car. The top five were neatly stuffed into the backseat when Charles returned, took my arm, and guided the baby and me to the car.

The streets of Detroit were a mess. We hadn't far to go but at least six additional inches had accumulated along Eight Mile Drive. If the plows had been there, it hadn't been recently. Despite the triple-treaded tires, we still slipped from side to side through choppy drifts; the thickness of the powder had been massaged by the traffic before us. Now and then, we'd catch a bare spot of pavement, when the car would lurch as the chains caught the ice-covered asphalt, causing my heart to leap into my throat, as I clutched the baby tighter. On one of those bare spots, a link of a chain let go; suddenly we were shocked by the sound of a bass drum, as the inside of a fender was struck by a flying chain with every revolution of the wheel.

"I have *Jiffy Links* in the trunk," said Charles.

He might as well have suggested that we put on bathing suits and head for Hamtramck, an area of Detroit with largely a Polish heritage. Or to Belle Isle, an island in the Detroit River used for recreation. I wanted to go nowhere but home. Stopping for anything, much less to repair a broken chain at midnight on Christmas Eve was not a part of my plan, assuming I had one.

"What will happen if you don't fix it?" I asked.

"It'll drive you crazy with the bang, bang, bang as the chain hits the fender."

"Will it ruin the fender?"

"It might dent it a little."

"Will it ruin the tire?"

"Doubtful. It will be annoying; nothing more."

"Take us home," I demanded. "These six little people need to be fast asleep before Santa arrives."

"Has he come yet?" asked Jocey. The jabbering in the backseat stopped while five pairs of eyes searched the back of my head for an answer, and five pairs of ears pointed forward, eager to hear an affirmative response.

"I don't know. Let's ask Daddy to turn on the radio to see if there is any report of where Santa is now."

There was a chorus of agreement. After a few seconds of listening to *WJR*, there it was— "The North American Aerospace Defense Command—NORAD in Colorado Springs—has Santa Claus on radar. Santa and his reindeer have been located over eastern Canada. He has Newfoundland, New Brunswick, and Quebec to visit, after which he will concentrate on the New England states and eastern New York. He is expected to be over Detroit sometime after three a.m. in the morning. Stay tuned for later bulletins. This is the North American Aerospace Defense Command—NORAD in Colorado. And now back to your regular programming."

As *WJR* shifted out of bulletin mode and began to play *The Flying Purple People Eater*[1], Scotty asked, "The Purple People Eater isn't going to eat Santa Claus, is he?"

Charles laughed. "No, I don't think so. Somehow, Santa manages to make it to the home of every good girl and boy before sunup. I think he'll be able to find our white bungalow on Evergreen Avenue."

---

[1] The Flying Purple People Eater was a Number One hit song in 1958. Here is the first verse:

 Well, I saw the thing comin' out of the sky
 It had the one long horn, one big eye
 I commenced to shakin' and I said "ooh-eee"
 It looks like a purple people eater to me.

Scotty breathed a sigh of relief that only a six-year-old can understand. The loot was on its way. Yes, there was a package out on the front unheated porch under the tree. He'd like to see what was in it. Each of the children had one present that we had placed under the tree on the closed-in porch. Only Scotty had been promised his gift the night before Christmas, and that was because he knew what it was.

Scotty was counting the minutes as the miles rolled by much too slowly, to the constant *bang, bang, bang* of the broken tire chain. "I'm gonna open that box tonight!" he declared.

"I'll make you a deal," I said over my shoulder.

"What's that?"

"It's too cold to stand out on that porch tonight. If you'll go to bed when we get home, I promise to get you up before the others. We'll take the box inside tonight where it's warm, then I'll get you up at five, a half hour before everybody else, so you can open it then. Is that a deal?"

"Can't I open that tonight?" he asked.

"Deal?" I could be insistent, too.

With a dejected tone in his voice, and no doubt a dejected countenance, Scotty responded simply, "Deal." He exhaled loudly, that he might impart his dissatisfaction with his mother's offer, but sat back in the seat and, now less excited, dropped off to sleep.

In another fifteen minutes, we arrived home. Charles picked up speed as he moved down the street, allowing him to *gun* the car as far as possible up into the driveway. The land on Evergreen Avenue is relatively level, with but the barest incline from street to home. Placing the car closer to the building made transfer easier, of course, but most of all, kept the car from being buried in the snow thrown up when the plow moved along the city street.

The accumulated snow now formed a barrier that said *you've made it home. Don't push your luck. Any further and you'll have more to shovel to get back to the street in the morning.* Charles turned off the lights, killed the engine, climbed out of the car, and then came around to my side. He reached into the backseat, cautioned the older children to watch Shirley, and then scooped Cathy into his arms. Leaving us there, he walked to the front door, opened it, turned on the porch light, and put her in the living room. He then returned, opened my car door, helped me with the baby, and got us started. Finally, he scooped up Shirley, and invited the older children to follow closely, hanging onto his jacket.

Chapter 1: Christmas Eve

<u>Evergreen Avenue, Detroit, Michigan</u>

Shortly, we all were stomping the snow from our boots out on the porch. We then climbed into the house, which had become chilly. While I undressed the children and got them into their PJs, Charles stoked the coal-fired furnace, located just to one side of the kitchen of this one-story bungalow, with a block of coke briquettes. When the coke caught, the boiler began to make its usual clanging noise. Soon steam was escaping from the radiator. It would take a while for the house to warm. The furnace would have to be fed again about five a.m., so I was careful to tuck each of the children securely under a blanket or comforter.

Charles and I spent the next two hours assembling things that were "simple enough for a child to build," wrapping every secret in its own gaily-decorated disguise.

***

They told me at the inquest that Charles died instantly. Though I was initially convinced that was so, something happened to lead me to think otherwise, and I'll share that later in the story. This is what I remember.

It took more than a half hour to settle the kids in for the balance of the long wait for Santa Claus. Adrenaline seemed to be coursing through the veins of the older five children. The baby had no idea what was happening, so Jason was changed and bedded in his crib, where he quickly fell asleep. Despite knowing we'd be up for most of the rest of the night, Charles' priority was a beer and a quick look at the television for the scores of the *Redwings'* game.

"After that harrowing drive home, I think I deserve a drink."

On the way home, I'd promised to pour him a *Stroh's*, and he wasted no time enlisting Donny to pass the demand once we'd arrived.

"Momma, Daddy wants a beer," demanded the five-year-old in his most mature and tired voice.

"Tell him to get his own beer," I replied, annoyed that with the kids to undress from the storm and to get into pajamas, the lout could think only of himself. To ensure that the message was delivered, I shouted to my husband from the bedroom: "Get your own beer. I'm busy."

With a groan, Charles rose from the overstuffed chair and said, "All right, all right. But you *promised*!"

"If you're so desperate for a beer at this hour, I'll get one for you just as soon as the children are all nestled in their beds, with visions of sugar plums at least advancing on sleepy land," I shouted. "And I could certainly use a hand with Donny. He's ricocheting off the walls. You can get the score from *The Free Press* in the morning." I turned my head and hurled my voice toward the boys' bedroom, just off the kitchen beside the pantry. "Settle down in there! Your father is gonna get you!"

Charles popped his head into the master bedroom. "You know, Denise, *you* are precisely why I never joined the Army. One drill sergeant in my life is quite enough."

I looked up, grinned, and spoke in my best drill sergeant voice: "Count your blessings, doughboy. We're between wars—the last one in Korea and the next one somewhere else on God's green planet. We've been busy for more than seven years accumulating more deferments than you could possibly ever need. The trade-off is that in exchange for wriggling on your belly across some forsaken field of disputed land, all you must do is to help get a few kids ready for bed. And, good sir, I would remind you that you have miles to go before you sleep, making sure that a certain expected visitor has milk and cookies waiting on the cold porch."

Charles popped the smartest salute his untrained hand could produce. "Aye, aye, Ma'am, Sir. I will see to the bed patrol forthwith. But I'm gonna do it with a beer in hand. Can I get one for you?"

"Maybe later," I said. "When we've filed all these deferments away, I'll brew a pot of coffee. You'd better start hauling the loot down from the attic."

***

He disappeared after that. Because the house had been especially cold, he dropped another package of coke briquettes into the furnace, tossed in some crumpled newspaper, and stirred the coals. The three girls had been sleeping in our room for a few days now, because it was just too cold in the back bedroom. Tonight was no exception. We'd moved their beds, resolving that once it began again to warm, they would be evicted to their own room. The baby's crib was in the boys' room.

Charles and I stayed up to watch the hockey game, coming from Seattle, while we worked on the gifts. He did, anyway. I went to bed before the game ended. I didn't sleep well because the house was cold. The repairman from the realty company had been out the day before to work on the furnace, but it was still not heating the house.

During the night, the wind picked up and the snow continued to fall. Accumulation that night would hit fifteen inches, and where the snow drifted between the houses on the street, there were drifts of the white stuff to four or five feet.

As promised, we brought Scotty's *Lionel* train in from the cold porch. We had put it unwrapped under the tree, since he was with us when we bought it and he knew about it. It had sat there for a week. Tonight, we would wrap it along with the new mittens and socks, undershirts, briefs, and the pint-sized hockey stick with the *Redwings* logo stamped on it. Clever people, the Japanese.

Clothes in the next size up—the oldest boy just doesn't get hand-me-downs from an older sister—a ring-toss set, and a black hockey puck rounded out the assortment destined to delight Scotty's eyes. Because we knew he wanted to play hockey and had outgrown his skates, we had a pair of the nicest boys' hockey skates we could afford, and Charles had gotten them sharpened. We expected that during the afternoon Scotty would be out on the ice in the backyard, facing down the most formidable on-ice forward he could find, Sam the Beagle, who just loved to chase anything that skidded across the frozen yard.

Three dozen presents and at least two cups of coffee each later, except for the train and Jocey's porcelain doll, the wrapped packages were once again back on the enclosed front porch awaiting the local rooster, which in our case, was the *ding, ding, ding* of the *Big Ben* alarm clock, set for five o'clock. We made sure the clock was shut off during its slow ring phase, because if it ever got to the end of its cycle, the resulting cacophony is more than enough to jar your fillings. Of course, the plan was that only two of the children would be getting up early with us. The reality was that three more would be padding around the house once it began to stir.

I rolled over and turned the irritant off. With a well-placed thumb to Charles' ribs, I commanded, "You gotta get up, you gotta get up, you gotta get up in the morning," in a singing voice nearly as annoying as the clock. Irving Berlin had nothing on me. "Roll it out, doughboy. It's cold in here. Toss something onto the fire. We've got a busy morning ahead of us."

I rose, dragged on the long johns, denim pants, and shirt that rested on the back of the vanity chair, slipped into my house slippers, spoke again to my husband, and stood there long enough to know that he was in motion. Then I stumbled, bleary-eyed, to the kitchen.

I prepared a small pot of coffee, plugged it in, put a pan of water on the stove, and lit the burner. The kids would welcome hot chocolate on this cold Christmas morning. I moved slowly into the frigid bathroom and stayed just long enough to brush my teeth. There would be no shower this morning, but I wasn't about to greet the children with "morning breath."

When I returned to the kitchen, the water was hot and the coffee was done. I ripped open two packets of cocoa and dumped them into cups. Then I poured the two cups of coffee and was moving toward the front room picture window when Charles emerged from the bedroom looking extremely unkempt.

I handed him a coffee and said, "I'm gonna check the snow. You get Scotty up." Why I even bothered to say that, I don't know. It was after five a.m. and pitch-black outside.

I couldn't tell the depth of the snow. The streetlights were on only at the ends of the block in both directions; the ones that would have illuminated our front yard had been out for more than a month. Apparently, snow removal was more important to the City of Detroit than changing the light bulb in front of my house.

There was enough light, however, to see that the plows had crossed behind the car, creating a wall of street snow that would have to be moved before we had any hope of going to my mother's for Christmas Day dinner. For a moment, I savored the idea of curling up with a rum and eggnog, with a stick of cinnamon floating on the top.

I awakened Jocey by shaking her gently. When she opened her eyes, I put my finger to my lips and whispered, "Santa has been here. There's a box in the living room with your name on it."

Her feet hit the floor and after a small search, both feet found their way into slippers.

"Want a hot chocolate?" I asked. She nodded her assent. From the kitchen, I could hear the male voices. Scotty didn't know which was more important, his hot chocolate or his train. Further, he had found among his gifts a toy gun with a holster and a pair of cowboy boots, all of which he had put on immediately. Working my way back into the kitchen, it looked as if he were just about to capture some bad guys. If he only knew....

"Did you build the fire?" I asked Charles, still focusing through bleary eyes at a bathrobe-clad man whose hair desperately needed combing.

"Sure did. The steam is building and you should have knocks in the radiators in mere minutes."

***

The smell of coffee permeated the house. Charles had tossed three of the coke brick units into the boiler and stoked the fire. The four older children and I were up by 5:30 a.m. on Christmas morning.

Scotty and his dad decided to assemble the train in front of the furnace since it was warmer there. Jocey and Donny were in the living room opening their gifts. Shirley and Jason were still in bed. Cathy was with me in the dining room, attempting to put on her shoes, her *Mary Janes*.

I went into the front room to watch Jocey open and exult about her porcelain doll, fully aware that what she was most interested in was a toy typewriter, which had now been brought into the house from the porch.

Shirley had left her bed—the one she shared with Cathy—and had moved to the lower bunk in the boys' room, closer to the heat, and of course still snug from the warmth that Scotty had left. She took no note of Jocey and me—or the doll. She took no note of the cup of hot chocolate on the floor beside Scotty. She was still tired, and cold, and to Scotty's bed, she went.

The intent was eventually to mount the three-rail *Lionel* track to a piece of plywood, where Scotty and his father could build a small community. But today—Christmas Day in the wee hours—the idea was to get the oval-shaped track assembled, the transformer and control mounted, and the engine and cars mounted so they could begin to operate.

The *boys*—father and son—worked on the project together. Eventually the engine, the tender, and the two cars that had come with the set began to work, and the two of them had slipped into a fantasy of their own. As Scotty knelt and worked the control, Charles stood back to survey their handiwork.

The fire had been heating the water in the boiler for nearly an hour. It had begun as warm water anyway, but the addition of the three coke bricks had built a head of steam, coursing into the pipes and the radiators. Yes, indeed, they would have to be bled.

The last words that Charles ever said were, "I thought Santa was bringing a bigger train to Scotty."

I answered, "Next year Santa will bring Scotty and his dad a larger train." The explosion interrupted my sentence.

***

When Charles heard noises from the furnace, he turned his attention away from the train and his son, intending to open the furnace door to see what was making them. He never made it. Now with nearly a full head of steam, the boiler in this little house blew open, picking Charles up and throwing his body over his son and into the adjacent room. Later examination would show that he had been propelled into the kitchen range with sufficient force to impress the shape of his head on the oven door.

The lights went out. We were in total darkness, except near the furnace, from which clouds of steam were escaping, and the small fire in the firebox. Charles was dead; killed instantly.

I ran to the door, grabbing Jocey and Donny as I passed. I took them to the front yard and told them to stay there and not to come back in the house, no matter what they saw or heard. There wasn't a soul in the street. It was pitch-black. Because neighbors had heard the blast, lights were beginning to come on up and down the street. To anybody who could hear, I screamed, "Call the Police! Call the Fire Department!"

***

Jocey was more than eight years old, and while her frequent care for her brother Scotty wasn't strange, this was certainly nothing she had ever encountered. He was crying because he was hurt; she was crying because she was scared. She wanted to stay in the house with her mother.

I now became commanding: "You keep your brother out on the lawn and stand in the snow. Get as far away from this house as you can. Hold his hand until I come out. If you don't, I will spank you both."

It was certainly an idle threat but was the only discipline I could muster on short notice at six in the morning, in the dark, in a house that could very easily blow up any minute. As it was, the blast had shattered most of the windows, and cold air was rushing through the house.

I now had to focus my attention on finding the other children. Children one and two were accounted for. I could only pray that I could find three, four, five, and six quickly. Child number six was easily located—in the master bedroom in his crib, crying. For the moment, he wasn't going anywhere.

Back in the house, as I ran toward Scotty's voice, I tripped over Cathy. She was unconscious, so I picked her up and ran out into the front yard and placed her in the snow. That move would prove to be fortuitous. I put Cathy down between Jocey and Donald and counted noses. Three down, three to go.

Again, I ran toward Scotty's voice. While I had some concept of where he was, it was dark. He was sitting on the kitchen floor, his back against a wall. When I started to lift him, I found that Charles' body pinned the boy. Quickly, I moved Scotty's legs together and formed my arms on the side of his legs as a splint. Because I had medical training, I was aware that there might be other injuries, and did this to protect him. When Scotty was loose, I gathered him into my arms, ran from the house, and put him with the other children in the snow. Again, a count: one, two, three, four. Four in the snow; two yet in the house.

Next would be the baby—I knew exactly where he was—in the crib. I grabbed him up in a blanket and ran outside, putting Jason with the other children. Again, a count: five accounted for—one more to find.

The house now—in addition to being completely dark—was eerily silent. I'd seen Shirley move into the boys' room, but as I entered the room, the debris of the collapsed wall and the fractured bunk bed was everywhere. I got down on my knees and crawled, calling for my daughter. She was beneath a mattress that covered her when she'd been blown across the room. I grabbed her and headed for the door. As I got to the door, someone took the child from my arms. The firefighters and police had arrived.

Out on the lawn, those who were not injured were in shock. An ambulance had arrived, and cars with flashing lights were beginning to move up Evergreen Avenue from Gratiot Avenue. I remained in the house.

***

The concept that my husband had just died was foreign. I shouted Charles' name and heard nothing. While it was indeed dark, there was enough light reflected from the now open firebox for me to recognize he was going nowhere. I went to his side, shook him briefly, and ran my hand under his back. He was gone. Having spent so many years working in a hospital, I knew death when I saw it. I staggered into the living room and sat on the couch, relieved that the authorities were here.

I was in shock with no thought as to my next step. Then came the realization that my children were outside in the snow. My kids! I had to get to my kids! I rose to move toward the door and was blocked by the Fire Captain, who asked, "Is there anybody else in the house?"

Pointing toward the kitchen, I said, "My husband is on the floor in there." The Captain and another fireman turned to move toward the kitchen. "Don't bother," I said. "He's dead."

"Get her out of here," commanded the Fire Captain. Another firefighter moved to take my arm, but I wrested it away. I was becoming disoriented; it seemed ludicrous that they were going to the kitchen. Charles was dead! Why bother? In my mind, I rehearsed the scene: *I told you! He is dead!* It didn't make sense that they didn't listen.

***

The disorientation continued. I rose and leaned against the living room wall, trying subconsciously to hide in a corner, shielding myself from the gigantic hurt that had just been thrust upon me. From the kitchen, the two firefighters returned, carrying Charles' body beneath the arms and the knees. His head was rolled back.

I screamed.

"My God! Is she still in here?" shouted the Captain. "Get her out of here!"

A police officer officer gently took my arm to usher me from the house, attempting to shield my view of Charles' body. He was not successful. I saw everything.

The firefighters placed Charles' body on the floor of the closed-in porch and waited for a gurney to be brought from an ambulance that had arrived on the scene. For the first time since the explosion, I had a view of what the explosion had done to my husband.

Outside there were police cars and a single ambulance, the only one stationed at the nearest fire station. I was becoming increasingly confused, especially when I discovered that the five children I'd deposited in the snow were gone! I was in a state of panic. "Where are my kids?" I screamed. I ran to the street and looked up and down. I stumbled through the ankle-deep snow towards the ambulance. The kids *had* to be in the ambulance. But they weren't!

Again, I screamed, "Where are my kids? A police officer directed me to one of the cruisers. My children were in the backseat of the car, I was told. However, of my six children, only three—Scotty, Shirley, and Jason were there.

"Where are the others?" I screamed. Hysterics had set in. They must have gone back into the house. I started in that direction, when a burly police officer stopped me to say that the other kids were not hurt and had been taken in by the next-door neighbor. The three children in the cruiser needed to go to the hospital immediately.

The burly police officer took me by the hand and started walking toward the car.

I panicked. There was no way I was going anywhere without all six kids. I began to fight against the officer, twisting to get away from him. In the scuffle, I grabbed his watch with enough force to tear it from his wrist.

When I woke up, I had a sore jaw and was in the cruiser with my three shocked and silent children, on our way to Saratoga Hospital.

Ahead, in the ambulance, the body of Charles Butler Bennett led the way.

Chapter 2: Prelude to Christmas

Detroit, Michigan, 1958

You've met my family, more or less. Charles Butler Bennett and I met in elementary school when I was nine. He was four years ahead of me. We began to date during high school when I was fifteen, in 1948.

At age sixteen, I managed to get pregnant and announced that to my parents. They were not amused. On July 7, 1950—five days before my seventeenth birthday—our first child, Jocelyn Barbara Bennett came into the world. I brought Jocey, as I would come to call her, back to my parents' home. One month later, on August 7, Charles made an honest woman of me.

Mother could accept, albeit with much comment and protest, nearly anything—other than an illegitimate child. We were married in the Grace Baptist Church of Van Dyke, Michigan, a suburb of Detroit. Mother arranged that, since she didn't want it known to the priest who headed the local Catholic Church that her only daughter had a stain on her soul. Now there were three of us in need of a place to stay, and Mother made available an apartment among the rentals she owned. This would be the beginning of Mother's dominance, which I resolved to overthrow.

Charles got a job on the assembly line at Chrysler's Dodge plant in Detroit, but with little seniority, the ephemeral nature of the automaker's employment always kept us a step or two off balance. While mother was consistently there to help, she *always* made known the cost of the help and how she felt life ought to be for her daughter.

Scott Allen Bennett arrived at the end of June in 1952, to be followed by Donald Hefka Bennett in August of 1953. We might have stopped there, but Catholics are known to be good breeders, and Charles Butler Bennett was a good Catholic breeder with considerable DNA to contribute. Of course, he had a willing partner. We both knew what caused these four-limbed wailing machines; we just never could get the rhythm. Catherine Jean came in October 1954; Shirley Louise in October of 1955; and finally Jason Paul arrived in February of 1958. If there is a pattern to this activity, note that there was only one cold-weather pregnancy. We knew that the cold hadn't caused them. Have you ever been pregnant in the hot summer humidity? It's no fun!

***

We'd been married for slightly more than eight years when we bought the bungalow and living in Mother's apartment. By that time, Chrysler had begun to cut back to do one of its many reorganizations, including the Dodge Division. Charles was in and out of work on a regular basis. Because of the instability of Charles' job, he worked until September of 1950. He quit when we married; when we came back from our honeymoon, he applied at General Motors in Livonia, where he worked as a spot welder on automobile transmissions.

By sheer coincidence, that factory burned down on the night of Donny's birth, and for a short time, Charles was again out of work.[2]

His job was union-protected, so we were not without income. Shortly thereafter, GM bought Ford's factory at Willow Run and moved its operation there, where Charles continued to weld.

In 1955, Charles was diagnosed with esophageal (throat) cancer. A lifelong smoker, he now had a death sentence of his own making. In those days, chemotherapy didn't exist; there was only radiation treatment by X-Ray. Charles was scheduled for twenty sessions of treatment over a three-month period. He managed sixteen sessions, when it was discovered that he had radiation poisoning.

He began to miss work, taking sick leave. Because his job was protected, he continued to receive money, so we were still able to live comfortably. For some time, I worked as an EKG and Operating Room Technician at the Holy Cross Hospital in Detroit. I would later achieve my nursing degree from Johns Hopkins Nursing School.

***

After living in several apartments made available by my mother, we decided to find a way to buy a house of our own.

Charles had a predilection of his impending death. He'd expressed his feelings in three short statements: "I know

---

[2] AUGUST 12, 1953. The General Motors Transmission factory in Livonia, MI, was destroyed by a fire begun when a welder's torch ignited an oily rag that was dragged through the facility on a conveyer belt. The loss is one of the greatest disasters in American business—$50 Million.

your family will destroy you," "I'm alive; I can't bear to think about your remarriage," and "I'll never see my children grown." The house was Charles' way of providing stability for his family after he was gone. Who would have known that I'd feel guilty for having insisted on the house—*this* house?

It was listed in the Saturday real estate pages of *The Free Press:*

> **Three bedroom home on secluded Evergreen Avenue west of Gratiot in East Detroit. Buy direct from the realtor. Low down payment. $16,500. Listed by the Anderson Kane Real Estate Agency.**[3]

There was also a picture of a small white frame house.

A telephone call put us in touch with the realtor. I knew the area, so location wasn't a problem. There were good schools in the area for my oldest two. Public transportation was close enough for me to catch a bus to the hospital. It was forty miles from Willow Run, and Charles could carpool with several other men.

At first, everything looked perfect. The down payment was a major concern, however, so Charles could see the joy on my face when I learned that it was only five hundred dollars! I made an appointment for us to see the place the next afternoon.

We looked over the house and agreed to take it. On the following Monday, I drew that money from our meager

---

[3] I find no current reference to Anderson Kane Real Estate Agency currently in the Detroit area. It may be defunct. There is, however, a Kayne Anderson Real Estate Investment firm of Boca Raton, Florida. I do not know if they are related.

savings—with six kids, there wasn't much—and had a cashier's check made to the realty company. Tuesday was a day off for Charles, so we met with the realtor early that morning.

What I didn't realize at the signing was that there was no bank involved in financing the house. Because the agent owned the house, the papers we signed gave us only a *contract* on the house. It was a chattel mortgage. It wasn't customarily applied to property or buildings, but in practice, it was used by property owners who wished to maintain title and recognized that the buyer might not be able to obtain financing.

We made monthly payments directly to the agent, in whose name the deed was registered. It benefited the agent; if we defaulted or left, we had no title in the house, the chattel would be forfeited, and the agent was legally able to keep what had been paid on the house. The obverse was also true. If faced with leaving, there was no lingering financial obligation. That was the one stroke of good luck for my family in this story. It was the only way justice was delivered against this landlord. We moved in—all eight of us—on October 15, 1958.

The house was smaller than a thousand square feet. While it had three bedrooms, as advertised, the smallest was little more than a walk-in closet. For the moment, that suited Jocelyn, Catherine, and Shirley just fine. We could foresee the time we'd have to build a room in the attic, as Jocey became older, and would want a room of her own. The middle-sized bedroom could comfortably accommodate three. The two boys were in there in bunk beds. We fully expected that in a few months, Jason would be their roommate. We could see ourselves outgrowing that house in a few years. By that time, it might have been possible financially, if Charles didn't succumb to cancer.

The house looked like its picture. The floor plan had a living room with a picture window to the left of the door, the master bedroom to the right, a dining room, a kitchenette, a bathroom back in the cold part of the room, and a pantry. In the pantry was installed a coal-fired furnace and a two hundred gallon boiler, connected to an eighty gallon hot water tank in the attic. The pantry provided space for food and household tool storage, plus a small walk-in closet.

The furnace's firebox protruded through the wall into the kitchen, offering the openings through which coal might be shoveled and ashes removed. The furnace hadn't been converted to oil, and there was no basement in which to store coal. We contented ourselves with the purchases of battery-sized blocks of coke, anthracite from which gas has been extracted. The wall to the left of the furnace abutted the boys' bedroom. To gain maximum warmth, we had pushed the bunk beds against the common wall.

There was a shed in the back yard. Despite the temperature, Charles stored our lawn mower there. It would be useful next spring. We had some other things that belonged in that shed, as well. Sam and Henry, Charles' Beagles, needed a place to stay, and the shed was suitable for the daytime.[4]

---

[4] Sam 'n' Henry was a radio series performed by Freeman Gosden and Charles Correll that aired on Chicago radio station WGN from 1926 through 1928. The ten-minute program is often considered the first situation comedy. Gosden and Correll reworked the premise on a more ambitious scale to create their long-running radio show *Amos 'n' Andy*. Source: Wikipedia.

We generally brought them in at night, but for some reason, we didn't on Christmas Eve. The houses on each side were separated from ours by common shrubbery that kept us from looking into the others' bedrooms. Good fences make good neighbors, they say, but dense shrubbery works too.

Our lot was separated from the house behind us by a chain link fence that spanned the property. We couldn't put the dogs into the back yard without a retaining fence, however, and one doesn't install postholes in frozen ground. So, we bought a chain-link kennel enclosure and installed at the front of the shed. Charles installed a *doggie door* in the shed and put blankets inside in the space prepared for them. We had no concern that they would dig beneath the fence since the ground was frozen. That didn't stop them from trying, however.

The inside of the house was nothing spectacular. There were hardwood floors throughout, except for the kitchen and the bathroom, which had standard utility linoleum. We couldn't afford carpeting, so we made do with throw rugs and cautioned the kids not to go barefooted. Had the house been built on a slab, it might have been warmer, but it had been built on piers, and there were concrete steps into the front door from the street. There was enough crawl space beneath the house to allow a thin person to wrap the water and sewer lines with heat tape.

The walls of the inside rooms were as white as the exterior of the house. The addition of color to at least the inside of the home would begin in the spring if I had anything to say about it. Eight years of that kind of decoration was enough. It was time for this building—this house—to be my home.

I could see that shelf space would be needed to accommodate the books stashed in boxes in the attic. I could also see that each of the bedrooms could use something better for clothing storage. Charles was handy enough to build many things, but I didn't envision him standing out in the snow in freezing weather cutting shelves and building toy boxes. That could wait until the crocuses began to peep from the grass, and that would no doubt have to be mowed sometime in April or May. We had no idea what the lawn would be—it was October and there was snow on the ground, so we didn't care. We had a house of our own, one that didn't require obeisance to my mother.

We would discover that the house was not well insulated. October was cold and early winter flurries were frequent. The back bedroom was too cold to sleep in, so we dragged two of the girls' beds into the master bedroom, put the two youngest girls in one of them at opposite ends, and gave Jocey her own space.

Even the master bedroom, "master" merely by comparison with the other rooms, could barely accommodate a standard double bed, a dresser, and a chair. Now there were two additional beds in the room. Both the large bedroom and the boys' room were close to the furnace, and so they were the first beneficiaries of the steam that left the boiler.

From the beginning, we had problems obtaining heat from the furnace. While we could get a fire going, there were problems with the boiler, which we brought to the realtor's attention. He'd get a man right on it, he said.

I was impressed that the realtor's operation was sufficiently successful that he could employ trade specialists. Only later did I discover that while he may have had a foreman, the workers were day laborers who were picked up every morning on Detroit's inner streets.

Such was the case of the man they sent to work on our furnace. He was obviously of French-Canadian extraction and his understanding of English was marginal. Two days before Christmas, the foreman showed up with François in tow. Mr. Foreman had, the day before, diagnosed our "lack of heat problem" as a steam valve that failed to open. When he and François arrived, they carried a tray of plumbing tools and short pieces of pipe, known as *nipples*, of varying lengths. Half in English, half in Canuck French, Mr. Foreman described the task that François was to accomplish, set the man to work, told me that he'd be back mid-afternoon to check on the man and to "inspect" the job he'd done—then left.

I knew nothing about furnaces or plumbing, so I had no idea whether François was competent to do the job. François, however, had no such misgivings. He turned to me and said a single word: "Hose?" After two or three attempts to understand, including some graphic gestures of his watering flowers, I finally got the message. I knew we had a hose, and were it summertime, it would no doubt be hanging out in the shed. It was in one of three-dozen boxes somewhere up in a dark attic; I wasn't about to go looking for it.

He shut off the water valve that supplied the boiler and asked if I had a pan. I found a three-quart saucepan and a pail for him to use, and he went back to the pantry, sat on the floor, opened the tap, and proceeded to drain—and dump in the kitchen sink—all two hundred gallons of water. Fortunately, the fire had gone out, but since we were halfway through October, I had serious doubts about having either heat or hot water for more than a couple of hours.

When he was sure that the boiler was empty, he disassembled the discharge line that led from the boilers to the radiators. With children to care for and unpacking to do, I didn't stand over the man to observe his work. I wouldn't have understood what he was doing had I been there. He banged the pipes with wrenches, glued the threads, and reassembled a selection of the plumbing nipples in place of what he'd removed. When he was done, he began again to fill the boiler. While he waited, he went outside to smoke a *Players*. I should have suspected something right then: *Players* is a product of the English Imperial Tobacco conglomerate and is sold in Canada. François was a day laborer from Canada, and as far as he was concerned, he'd finished the job and wanted to get back to the labor hall.

While I knew nothing about plumbing, I did know that anytime you fool with a radiator, it is necessary to bleed the system of air. If he didn't do that, we were in for some serious heating system knocking. The water in the boiler was as cold as the system that fed it six feet beneath the middle of Evergreen Avenue. Not until it had been heated would it be possible to bleed the lines. François wasn't about to wait as long as that would take. He'd been paid for this job, and as far as he was concerned, this job was done and he could leave. Perhaps he could find another job for a few hours before he went back over the Ambassador Bridge. When I was in the bathroom, François gathered up the tools, put them all back in the tray, left them in the pantry, and quietly slipped out the front porch door.

Now I was in a quandary. I wasn't about to build a fire in that furnace until Mr. Foreman, or some other knowledgeable person, had examined François' work. I put on a sweater and put the kids' snow clothes on them, as we busied ourselves waiting for the follow-up visit.

Mr. Foreman arrived sometime after 4:30 in the afternoon, with one thing on his mind—he wanted to stop for the day. He was tired. He'd had to deliver and monitor the work of a dozen men like François. A cold beer, a hot supper, and watching whatever hockey game was on television were on his mind. He looked over François' work and pronounced it satisfactory. "You can build a fire in that furnace now, Miss," he said, oblivious to the Munchkins gathered around my ankles.

"How long will it take to get the steam up?" I asked.

"The better part of two hours."

"What about air in the line?"

"Yes, there will be air in the line and it will knock. I'll come back after Christmas and bleed the lines. It will be annoying, but you'll have heat." He wanted to leave. Tonight was Christmas Eve, and he had scheduled a visit from one of Santa's helpers from Dayton's[5] to spend the night.

---

[5] Dayton's was an American department store chain founded in Minneapolis, Minnesota in 1902 by George Draper Dayton. In 1969, the Detroit-based J.L. Hudson Company merged with the Dayton Company to form the Dayton-Hudson Corporation, adding 21 Michigan-based stores to the total. Dayton's was the parent of Target, opening the first Target in 1962 as the discount store version of Dayton's. Target eventually grew to become the company's dominant division. In 2000, Dayton–Hudson renamed itself Target Corporation. Source: Wikipedia.

"Do I have to build a large fire now?"

"No. Do you have plans for the evening?"

"We always spend Christmas Eve at my mother's house."

"Since you won't be here for the evening...." He paused, and then said, "I don't envy you. We're supposed to get another five inches of snow tonight." He continued, "Since you won't be here for the evening, build a small fire. That will allow the water to heat gradually and increase the pressure slowly. If you add to it tonight, keep the fuel level low. In the morning, you can build the fire to a higher level. You'll have to put up with a day of knocking, but I'll be here the day after to adjust the system. Agreed?"

I reluctantly agreed, though it would be fair to say that I wasn't comfortable with his answer. It would be unnecessary, I thought, to ask Mr. Foreman to stay until the water heated; besides, we were going to be out anyway. Perhaps Mr. Foreman was also a *Redwings* fan. I knew Charles intended to watch at least the last period tonight after we got back.

I thanked Mr. Foreman for helping us and told him that we would see him in two days. How I wish I'd made Mr. Foreman wait. He didn't want to, and, I didn't want it either. We had to be at Mother's by seven. All three of my brothers would be there with their annoying wives, my sisters-in-law.

___

Chapter 3: The Aftermath

Detroit, Michigan, December 25, 1958

Saratoga Hospital and Children's Hospital of Michigan at Detroit

The police officer had knocked me unconscious, placed me onto his shoulder, and carried me to the cruiser. He would contact me later to apologize for the treatment but held that a frantic mother was keeping severely injured children from treatment. I'd tried to get into the ambulance but had been told that my children were in the cruiser. The ambulance left, ahead of us, carrying Charles' body.

I wasn't out for long. I awoke to find myself in the cruiser, headed to Saratoga Hospital, a couple of miles away. An officer was holding Jason in the front seat. I was in the backseat with Scotty and Shirley, both severely burned and in shock. All three of the kids were strangely silent. Stress was now taking over my soul, and for the duration of the trip, I prayed audibly—the *Our Father* and the *Hail Mary*.

"Guys, we're in terrible trouble," I said to the two beside me. They had to be in pain, but if they felt the pain, shock had taken over. I had all I could do to keep from succumbing, myself. I knew that for now I had to hold things together. I could fall apart later, at a more convenient time.

The siren was blaring; traffic was moving to the side as we passed. In retrospect, it seemed like only seconds before we arrived at the hospital. The officer holding Jason was busy on the radio, alerting the hospital's emergency room of our impending arrival. Ahead of us went the ambulance, but Charles wasn't going anywhere. He would come second in the quest for attention.

Several doctors and nurses, nameless and now faceless messengers of mercy met us at the outer door of the emergency room. They didn't wait for gurneys; they gathered the children up and carried them into the building. I had somehow melted into the granite solidity that formed the walls of the hospital.

I could then—and I can now—see myself in toto, an out-of-body experience of sorts that signaled the beginning of what I now know as PTSD—Post-Traumatic Stress Disorder. Of course, its real beginning was back at the house following the explosion, when I functioned in fully automatic mode, and had backed into a corner in the living room, oblivious to everything except the rescue and protection of my children.

While time has allowed me to compartmentalize what happened and subordinate it to the process of living, the last sixty-plus years of my life have been one nightmare after another, following the nightmare of Christmas Day, 1958.

***

Things were happening away from the hospital, as well. The neighbor at the eastern side of my house had taken in three of my children. Jocey, Cathy, and Jason were there. Eight-year-old Jocey knew her grandmother's name and telephone number, so my mother was summoned and told that Cathy had burns on her left leg, which they found when they took off her pajamas. The area's only ambulance was on the way to the Saratoga Hospital. Another was unavailable.

My brother Fred and his family were visiting from Florida. Fred quickly arrived at the neighbor's house, picked up Cathy and headed for Saratoga Hospital. They arrived fewer than five minutes after our entourage, as I was pacing the hallway, worried sick about the condition of my children.

Shortly after that, as it developed, the police contacted my mother to announce that something should be done to secure the property. The fire department had sprayed the entire inside of the house—including all the closets—with fire-retardant foam. [6] [7]

***

At the hospital, some very caring ER attendants gave us immediate attention. They placed all four available children into adjacent rooms, but each lay on a gurney. I watched as each child was treated. I watched as one of the attendants removed Scotty's cowboy boots and holster, which he tossed onto the floor. Someone then picked them up off the floor and tossed them into the trash. After the funeral, a fireman returned the boots and holster, and I was amazed to see that the burn had been buffed out.

---

[6] We would learn that the fire department presence that morning at 16201 Evergreen Avenue involved one pumper, four fire trucks, one ambulance, the car of the fire chief, and nearly two-dozen firefighters. They ran 150 feet of 1.5" line, 550 feet of 2.5" inch line, and four hundred feet of 1" line, connected to the pumper, which was in turn connected to a hydrant further down the street. An explosion at that early hour on Christmas Day drew everybody's attention. Source: Fire Department Incident Report.

[7] A check at *Google Earth* shows no domicile at 16201 Evergreen Avenue. Apparently, the house was razed.

A nurse called attention to Shirley because she was bleeding from the ears. She had suffered a basal skull fracture.

I don't recall exactly who made the decision, but someone in charge advised me that the children were too seriously injured to be treated at Saratoga. They would have to be transferred to the Children's Hospital of Michigan at Detroit.

About the time I saw the blood oozing from Shirley's ear, I heard Cathy cry. Turning toward the sound of her voice, I saw her in Fred's arms. He was standing in the ER's hallway, holding Cathy. The doctor asked if she was injured, as Fred was handing her to a nurse. She was. The nurse took Cathy from Fred's arms and asked her name. She, like the others, would soon be transferred to Children's Hospital, where the burns to her left leg would be treated.

By this time, Charles' body had been examined and he had been declared as Dead on Arrival (DOA). A physician told me that I should identify the body before leaving for Children's Hospital, so it could be moved to the morgue. Fred agreed to do it, and as quickly as we had arrived at Saratoga, we were on our way to Children's Hospital, about ten miles away, all now carried in a single ambulance. Scotty and Shirley were on gurneys in the back of the ambulance. A fireman held Cathy and I held Jason. I was numb. I have no recollection where Donny was. Again, I had that out-of-body experience. I wasn't in that ambulance with six injured children: I was somewhere above looking at a family that was being rushed with sirens blaring to the Children's Hospital.

***

We were met at the Children's Hospital with the same sense of urgency and caring that we had experienced at Saratoga. Here, however, the staff was more attuned to the needs of small children, and several burn victims got their immediate attention.

The kids on the gurneys were wheeled into the ER. The others were carried into the hospital by ER staff. There were so many doctors, nurses, and technicians; they were too numerous to count.

Again, I found myself backed against the wall, as if somehow it was merely a scene to watch and not one in which I was a participant. I was conscious, but to some extent, I had regressed to infancy. I retreated into the woodwork while the team performed triage on my children.

Then somebody discovered that I was standing there barefooted. I can't recall now just where I lost my slippers, but it had to be in a snowdrift somewhere in front of the house. I had no idea how long I'd been walking in deep snow and below-freezing temperatures. I didn't feel cold and yet my feet were discolored. Nobody at Saratoga had noticed, but now one of the ER doctors did and asked if I was all right. I wasn't cold. In fact, I felt nothing; everything seemed surreal. They quickly found footwear for me.

Were it not for the tragedy, the scene might have been humorous. I couldn't talk. Someone found a cup of hot coffee for me. I was checked for obvious injuries. After the doctor checked my feet for frostbite, I was given a pair of hospital slippers. Then someone placed a blanket around me. I wasn't cold. In fact, I wasn't feeling anything. I can still see myself there in the ER of Children's Hospital, somewhat out of it, yet still communicative enough to react to the medical staff. Nobody addressed my need for treatment of shock.

Later that day I found a radio in the pocket of the Levis I was wearing. I've always loved music. I must have put it there when I got up that morning. It was a Christmas gift from Charles. He'd given it to me the night before, after the kids were in bed. I would never have known he bought it otherwise. He'd hidden it by the furnace. Charles never saw his gifts. He would have received them after the kids had opened all of theirs. I would ultimately put them in the casket with him.

Then the report: Scotty and Shirley were barely alive. The doctor told me that they were in severe shock from traumatic injuries, their blood pressures were low, their heartbeats were weak and rapid, and Shirley's pupils were slightly dilated.

From Saratoga Hospital, Fred went back to my mother's house with the news. I was there alone, and in no condition to make important decisions—yet I somehow managed during the nearly five hours we were there in the Emergency Room.

Cathy was burned on the leg but would fully recover. That was certainly good news. Jason appeared to be unharmed. He was given dry clothes and a bottle and put into a crib where I could see him. He was hooked up to oxygen long enough to clear his lungs. He'd be kept for observation until that afternoon and released. Fred returned to the hospital to take him home to my mother's house.

Each child had his or her own doctor and nurses. A portable X-Ray machine was brought in to examine Shirley's head. After the X-Ray, I was told that she was critical and was being transferred to one of the children's wards.

Shirley had oxygen, and an intravenous saline and water flow. She was given medication to stabilize her blood pressure. This was done immediately. She was in a coma and remained so for a month. She'd need extensive surgery, but it wouldn't be done until she came out of the coma. She was taken to the same room as her brother and wrapped in gauze dressings. She was not put into a *Stryker* frame—a common treatment for burn victims. Her head was stabilized by placing sandbags on each side.

Cathy was transferred upstairs. She had one seriously burned area that would require surgery. She was put into a ward with other children her age. She wasn't critical, but she would be operated on first.

Scotty's doctor said he was in the same condition as Shirley. Her burns were life threatening. She was burned over much of her body and would need extensive care. Scotty was in shock; he responded to pain but was not lucid. He and Shirley were put into a small room next to Cathy's ward. Nothing would be done for Scotty until he was stabilized.

***

Even though I was numb, I still somehow managed to complete the insurance and records forms. I am thankful that all the paperwork was an afterthought to the process. I wouldn't have been able to do so before somebody had attended the children. As I did that, and as I waited in the hallways and rooms, the doctors of the Children's Hospital of Michigan at Detroit ensured that I was informed.

Fortunately, for my condition, there were no decisions for me to make; I merely had to sign for the surgeries. At that time, I didn't experience flashbacks to the house; I was focused on the kids. People asked questions, but my answers were robotic. It was as if I weren't there. I wasn't talking; it was somebody else.

Jason was kept overnight for observation, and Fred picked him up on the following morning.

The three most seriously injured children were taken upstairs to their rooms after being stabilized as much as possible. There were doctors and nurses pushing a parade of gurneys. The kids were receiving oxygen; there were IVs running; and further treatments awaited them in a sterile room. Other doctors had been called back to the hospital. The doctors and nurses who had been treating the children in the ER surrounded Scotty's and Shirley's beds when they were discharged from the ER and sent to their rooms. Cathy and I followed, with other nurses pushing Shirley's bed.

Three children in hospital cribs, surrounded by a dozen doctors and nurses and me rushing along the deserted hallways must have been a scene found only in a combat zone, following 9/11 or some other disaster such as a bombing or plane crash.

It must have been nearing noon when we left the ER. Scotty was not put on the *Stryker* frame until sometime during the night.

I went with the nurses and Cathy, the least seriously injured child, who was put into a ward with other patients her own age. Scotty and Shirley were put into a room together and nurses were assigned to stay with them around the clock.

The Children's Hospital of Michigan at Detroit was a teaching hospital. Students from around the state came for training. Three senior students and one floor nurse together cared for them the first night. On the next morning, we obtained a private duty nurse to care for the two.

I was given a room next to the room that was used for Scotty and Shirley. The physicians asked me to hire private duty nurses for the children, because of their conditions. I hired three nurses from a Canadian hospital to cover the three shifts, plus a rotating nurse to fill in. That went on for the several months necessary until Shirley was discharged and Scotty was moved to a ward with healthier children his own age. Initially, Charles' medical benefits covered our expenses. Ultimately, their needs were covered by his life insurance.

In addition, I was told to start lining up blood donors because the children would require many transfusions. Fred owned a trucking company in Florida, and trucking companies employ Teamsters. It didn't take much to organize the local Teamsters to help; they donated blood the next day. They continued to be on call for donations for as long as they were needed. During the entire process, there was need for blood. He made the contact with a large man I knew only as "Peanut" from the Levi Trucking Company. The workers rolled up their sleeves and met our needs for the entire period. You can bet that I support the Teamsters.

Shirley's surgeries did not begin until she was awake and oriented. In addition to third degree burns over thirty percent of her body, she also had a depressed Basal skull fracture. She remained unconscious for nearly a month.

Shirley and Scotty had so many operations I truly don't remember the total. Skin grafts were done every two to three days for the first month or so. The operation that was to have been done to correct the depressed skull fracture was never needed. By the time Shirley was stable enough to withstand the operation, the depressed fracture had corrected itself. The skull was healing.

Cathy was burned on two percent of her body. After she recovered from the shock of the explosion, she was in fair condition. She was hospitalized for approximately six weeks, during which she was operated on and received several skin grafts. The grafts took and there were never any signs of infection. While the grafts healed, her left leg was splinted and she was required to wear diapers to keep her acidic urine away from the burned area. This was done to protect the new grafts. She tolerated the splint, but not the diapers. She had no intention to wear anything but panties.

One afternoon a nurse's aide came into her room, looking for me. Cathy had bitten the aide when she attempted to put the child into diapers. The aide asked me to speak to my daughter, so I talked to her and explained that she had to wear the diapers if she wanted to get well and go home. After that episode, we had no more biting. That changed her actions, but not her perspective. In essence, she was told that it would stay and she wasn't permitted to bite anybody.

I had only a short time to think about my surroundings before a surgical resident came to tell me that both Shirley and Scotty were in grave condition and that neither was expected to survive the night. He told me that Cathy would probably require surgery on her leg where it was burned. In the short term, however, she could go home.

When she was discharged a month later, my father came to pick her up and take her to his home. It was the first time Daddy had seen the children since the explosion. I stayed on at the hospital with Scotty and Shirley. They still needed many more surgeries, which meant more blood and various other treatments.

Once again, "home" became an apartment owned by my mother. Twice a week I went there to take a long shower, pack some clean clothes, and be with the other children for a couple of hours. By this time, Jocey, Donny, Cathy, and Shirley each knew that their father was dead. I think only Jocey fully knew what death really meant.

Jason appeared to be fine. He was sleeping. Oxygen had been ordered to help clean his lungs because of probable inhalation of smoke and dust. He would stay the night in the ER for observation. Would I please arrange for a family member take care of him after he was released the next morning? My mother and brother took him to mother's house on the day after Christmas.

***

After the papers hit the doorsteps, my mother's house was filled with every kind of gift one could imagine. By New Year's Day, the attic was filled from one end to the other with donations for the children and me. Some were slightly used items while others were new. There were some items still in holiday gift-wrap. There were unopened gifts from donors. There were dozens of envelopes, each with a card and money. As always, there is one bad apple in the barrel. When my husband's friend Mike went to get Charles' dogs the day after Christmas, someone had taken our tools and the lawn mower.

One day when I returned to the hospital, an attending physician was in the room that Scotty and Shirley shared. Scotty was in more pain than usual. I asked if he could give him something to ease the pain. He answered, "I won't allow your children to die in pain. If you ever see me give either of them a narcotic you will know there is nothing else I can do to help them." Watching them in pain was the hardest thing I've endured in my life. Watching day in and day out what they suffered was Heaven and Hell. I hated the pain but I knew it meant that there was still hope.

If you've never seen a burn patient, I sincerely hope you never experience one. When I first saw Scotty and Shirley in their room, I didn't recognize them. Shirley's face had a large burn from her lower lip into her lower cheek on the left side of her face. It was about the size of a silver dollar. This child, only three, whose head was of average size, had a burn the size of a silver dollar on her small cherub face. It was devastating to see. It is unbelievably hard when it is your child. She also had burns on her arms and legs.

***

For several weeks, it was touch and go. When I left their room, I never knew if I would return to find them dead. The longest time I spent away from the three of them for the first two months was when I attended Charles' funeral. Each night I returned to the hospital. In that two months' time, Shirley had more than thirty-five operations for skin grafts. Scotty had more than fifty. Cathy, far more fortunate, had one. I was anxious during every one of those surgeries, because they could die from being put to sleep. Every time one awoke was a moment of encouragement and relief.

After the funeral, I settled into the care routine established for the children. When the two sickest children were quiet, I would go to Cathy's ward and play with her and the other children. Often I would sit in one of the many available rockers and she and I would just rock and talk or sleep. She needed me also.

A private duty nurse was always in their room, so Scotty and Shirley were never alone. When the kids' nurse had to be out of the room for something, a floor duty nurse took her place until she returned.

At times, I would go down the street to attend Mass. At other times, I just walked around downtown Detroit. Friends and family would come to visit the children but they could not go into Scotty and Shirley's room for fear of infection. Only Cathy could have hands-on visitors. The top half of each patient's room was glass, so Scotty and Shirley's visitors could at least see them through the window. After a few weeks, most people stopped visiting the children. I understood and it didn't trouble me. If they didn't come, I didn't have to deal with them, despite their good intentions. They did what they could, but once the novelty wore off, it wasn't a pleasant experience even for the kids.

My most constant companion was my brother's girlfriend, Maude. She worked for a bank near the hospital. Every day after work, she would stop by. Maude was a wonderful person. I needed her so much. She was the only person besides me who was allowed in the room. On Saturdays and Sundays, she spent the weekends with us. When the kids were awake, she would talk to them. Often she or I would find ourselves on the floor under the *Stryker* frame talking to Scotty. If we were on the floor at that time, he could see us.

At times, the three of us would color in his books. One of us would be his hand and he would tell us which colors to use. At other times, we would read to him. One of the most life threatening conditions for gravely ill children is depression, so we did anything we could to prevent them from becoming depressed.

It was during one of these sessions that Scotty acknowledged that his father was dead. "Daddy's in Heaven, isn't he?" he asked. Now you know why I wonder if Charles had been killed immediately.

"How do you know that?"

"Daddy told me when I was lying with him on the floor. He told me not to worry; Mother would come and get me. He said not to worry; I could have his shotgun that he got for his birthday."

You can't tell me there wasn't a spiritual connection between the father and his son. I don't know exactly how, but one day I will.

The shotgun, by the way, though it was promised, was never given. It wasn't that Scotty didn't ask. He did but allowed that he wasn't old enough and agreed that I should give it to my brother.

Chapter 4: Adjusting to Reality

<u>Detroit, Michigan, 1959</u>

One day the nurse and I had been having a hard time keeping the IV running into Scotty's arm. We had propped it up with 4x4s (gauze pads). That didn't seem to help, so we took turns holding the needle at an angle that did work. The unit of blood was only half infused when Maude came into the room. When she saw what we were doing, she put on a doctor's gown and joined us. For the rest of the night, the three of us took turns holding that needle in place. The next morning, Scotty was off to surgery once again. After more than fifty operations, I gave up counting.

Scotty was burned on sixty percent of his body. Third degree burns on thirty percent of a six-year-old child's body are life threatening. Scotty had third degree burns on fifty percent of his body. Shirley had third degree burns on thirty percent of her body. They remained critical for two months.

The rapid loss of Scotty's body fluid caused his head and face to swell. He had burns on his face and on his torso, arms, and legs. Nearly his entire body was covered with dressings. The burn covering his forehead extended into his hairline and he lost part of his hair. On his one cheek, a moderately sized burn covered one of his beautiful dimples. He was on a *Stryker* frame so that he could be turned every two hours with as little pain as possible.

A *Stryker* frame looks like an ironing board mounted in a steel frame above and below padded sleeping boards. The padded board used while the patient in on his back is one continual board, placed on an axle that rotates. The padded board used when he was turned onto his stomach has an open space for his face. When turning the patient, nurses wrap sheets around the two boards with the patient sandwiched between and secured. The frame is turned with a crank; the top board is then removed, and the procedure is completed. When the patient is on his stomach, his only view is of the floor. I spent considerable time lying on a sheet on my back under the bed to talk with my severely burned son. Today's updated *Stryker* frame works by push buttons and jars the patient less.

***

Burn patients need frequent changes of dressing because of the constant oozing of blood and body fluids. It's a long procedure to change a dressing. The patient is put into a bathtub and the dressings are allowed to soak until they begin to loosen. The nurse, wearing sterile gloves, then removes the dressings very slowly. Some dressings close to the skin frequently stick, making the whole procedure most painful. Even after Scotty came home, the dressing changes continued. The bathtub was scrubbed with *Clorox* and plenty of hot water. Infection is one of the dangers of burns and one of the foremost causes of death among burn victims.

Scotty would sit in the tub and while he soaked, his brother Jason would play with him. When it came time for the dressing to be removed, Scotty would do that himself. He had started to remove the dressings himself while still in the hospital, after he was strong enough to sit up. Doing that part on his own seemed to be less painful for him.

Itching was another part of healing that was terrible for him. When he was finally home, rubbing his legs through the dressings to help stop the itching was a job Donny assumed. Scotty would be on a clean sheet on the floor; Donny would sit next to him and rub his legs for hours at a time. He never seemed to tire of caring for his big brother. Donny has never lost that desire to protect him. He is so much like his father in his attitude towards life.

Scotty's time in the hospital was not without amusement. Between surgeries, he was treated with topical creams, underwent debridement (the removal of dead skin), was covered in bandages, often put into a tub for the bandages to soak loose, and then unwrapped, during which time nerve endings were exposed.

One day the nurse, a black woman from Windsor, Ontario, Canada was soaking his dressings. She was using a highly polished stainless steel basin. She noticed Scotty looking at the pan and then at her. Where the swelling in his head had been, his skin had dried and blackened, and he could see his reflection in the pan. She laughingly told him he had not become a little black child. He would soon again be the same color as the rest of his family and me.

*****

While caring for my children was paramount, I still had a life to live, albeit there in the hospital. My clothes had been destroyed, so for the first few days I wore the same clothes and showered in one of the hospital's showers. The only thing to do was to shop. On one of my downtown trips with my sister-in-law, I outfitted myself with several sets of utility clothes.

I ate in the hospital cafeteria. As I transacted business, I kept my money in the hospital's safe—at one time, I had more than $8,000 in cash in their safe. After I'd spent ten days at my children's sides, I went home (for some time, my mother's house became "home") twice a week. Sadly, my mother never visited her grandchildren in the hospital, though both Scotty and Shirley spent months there.

The hours at the hospital were spent exclusively with the kids. For the time that each was in a coma, I talked gently to them. It is said that though they cannot react, they do hear. When they were awake, I moved to each and played with them. I would hold them and rock them. There was no time for me. I watched no TV. I read no books. I didn't even spend any time reading the *Detroit News*, which was the paper I normally received.

The hospital arranged for private duty nurses from the registry. I had to take care of the insurance paperwork and complete the paperwork from the nurse's registry. From the insurance settlement, I paid the private duty nurses.

People came and went during the four months we were there. There were teachers, friends, Charles' family, and others. My mother came in only three or four times during the four-month stay but would not visit the children. My father came in when Cathy went home. Maude was there, of course. David, my oldest brother, and his girlfriend came every night and often stayed until midnight.

***

Chapter 5: Family Composition

I was at court; I can't say I have any recollection of the event. While I wouldn't have remembered that, the loss of recollection is a serious part of the PTSD I experience; I've spent so many years suppressing the memories of Charles and the events of Christmas, 1958, that the scenes are not easily retrieved, and those that I can conjure are frightening to the extreme.

When my family moved into downtown Detroit in 1947, I transferred to St. Charles Catholic School. Because of local unrest, Mother chose to put me in parochial school. After that, I attended *Cass Technical High School*,[8] a college preparatory, scientifically focused school. I finished high school in May of 1950, turned seventeen in July, and married on August 7 of that year.

During high school, I worked as a soda jerk at a drugstore called Cunningham's. Few places nowadays, if any, have soda jerks, but in 1950, the job was a source of independence. I'd always wanted my own money.

When I was twelve, my family was offered a good price for the farm and sold it. Dad was a "gentleman farmer," and Mother was happy to be there until her mother died. After that, we moved twice—first to Garfield Street in East Detroit and then into Detroit itself. Back in Detroit, there were many places for a teenager to find work. I was usually

---

[8] Cass Technical High School (simply referred to as Cass Tech) is a public high school in Midtown Detroit, Michigan, United States. It was established in 1907 and is part of the Detroit Public Schools Community District.

at the top of my class, so working and studying was never a problem.

I had three brothers—David (1916-1972), born in Columbus, Ohio; Louis, (1929-1998), also born in Columbus; and Fred (born in Detroit in 1930) and I, born in Detroit. My father's parents were both originally from Kentucky. Dad moved to Columbus where he met and married my mother. Seeking better employment, they moved back to Michigan.

***

Although I can recall nearly everything about our marriage, most of my memory before then is not clear. What follows may seem random but are references to my life before Charles was killed.

Charles and I started dating when I was fifteen. We became engaged when I was sixteen and married when I was seventeen. I needed my father's permission. Charles was nearly twenty when we married; Michigan then needed no parental permission for the man. Mother was dead set against my marrying at that age generally and against my marrying Charles specifically. I solved that problem quickly by telling her that I was pregnant, and that unless she was looking forward to some sessions with the priest of our parish, she'd better go along. She did so reluctantly but made sure that during the early years of our marriage, she'd make our lives a living hell.

Charles had worked from age fifteen at labor-intensive jobs. At fifteen, he was a pinsetter at the *Colonial Bowling Alley* (long before automatic pinsetters). While I was at *Cass High School,* he got a job at an apartment complex located near the school, which allowed us to spend some unsupervised time together. After that, he went to Chicago, and I don't know what he did there.

One winter when I was about eight or nine and Charles was twelve, I taught him to ice skate. In those days, Hayes Street was not paved, and when it snowed and melted repeatedly, it would freeze and form a large sheet of ice. I was skating when Charles showed up. Since he had no skates, I went into the house, brought out my brother Louis' hockey skates, and the lessons began. They would be repeated for several weeks, until Charles became a good skater.

The next memory I have is of his cutting off the fingers and toes of *Betsy Wetsy*, one of my dolls. I was annoying him, so he did it maliciously. Years later, I told him that I'd married him to get even.

Since Charles was four years older than I, he played with my brothers more often. Charles and my brother Louis were the same age. Fred was a year younger. At the farm, on the "country side" of Hayes Street, we had three horses. The boys and an occasional neighbor would ride around the area, racing. This was during World War II and you didn't need a gas ration card for a horse.

I also recall one day when the boys, feeling mischievous, placed a call on the party line for the President of the United States, Franklin D. Roosevelt. They managed to get past the White House switchboard and to the President's secretary before the call was over. Others on the party line managed to snicker at the process, but the next day, when representatives of the FBI visited my parents, nobody in my house was snickering.

In those days, like many today, the mailboxes were lined up on the road. The boys got their jollies by killing skunks that somehow found their way to the mailboxes.

Although Charles and I were not always together, he usually knew where to find me. He was my keeper; from about age eight, he was always there for me. He protected. He counseled. In addition, I had a close girlfriend, Patti, my best friend, who lived across the street from my house. Patti was there also when I needed her. Patti will be intrinsic to the balance of this story.

Patti's father was in the Navy. She had two brothers. Jack was about the age of my oldest brother Doug and Don was the age of Fred. Patti and I were nearly inseparable and often I'd spend the night at her house. I called her mother "Aunt Betty" and her aunt, "Aunt Bee." Aunt Bee was staying with her sister's family because her husband was also in the military.

Aunt Bee had a son, Jerry, a few years younger than we were. We'd terrorize that little boy when we had to babysit for him. Patti's mother played the piano. There was a large upright piano in her living room; it was like one I had at home. We must have been about eleven at the time. When we were alone with Jerry, we would pull one end of the piano away from the wall, shove Jerry behind it, and push it back against the wall. We'd leave him there until almost time for Aunt Bee and Aunt Betty to return. At other times we would climb the large tree in her front yard, hide in the leaf-filled branches and spit on people who walked by. We were first-class troublemakers.

My father was an automotive engineer who worked for the Midland Steel [9] plant in Detroit.

The Midland plant had been converted into a war plant. Because it was a part of the World War II war effort, security was naturally high. During this time, my father was not at work because he'd been sick. However, he learned how important it was to call in, as two agents of the FBI showed up at the house to see why he hadn't been to work.

Hayes Street in the City of East Detroit was a dividing line between the city folk and the country folk. My family lived on the "country" side of the street. Hayes Street was unpaved at the time between Nine Mile Road and Ten Mile Road. On the "city" side were new houses, sidewalks, and modern structures that included garages. On the "country" side were farms (fifteen acres or more), with old farmhouses and barns, and no sidewalks. Power was run on the "city" side and it crossed the road to the farms. Water mains were laid the length of the street, in the middle. The houses had sewer service. The farms had septic tanks. If it cost money, and wasn't necessary, the farmers didn't want it.

Farming was done even on the "city" side of the street. Families on the "city" side often kept chickens in backyard chicken coops. Patti had a coop, as did I. Charles' family lived on the "city" side but had no chickens.

---

[9] Midland Steel began as Parrish and Bingham Company of Cleveland, OH--a manufacturer of trolley, wagon, and bicycle parts in 1894. With the introduction of the automobile, it began to make automobile frames, largely its primary business today. In 1923 it joined Detroit Pressed Steel Company and the Parrish Company of Detroit to form Midland. It supplied platforms and bodies, largely for Ford Motor Company. Midland was one of the few firms that had deep-draw presses capable of stamping out intricate contour body panels. During World War II, it was pressed into service to make frame rails for jeeps and hulls for the Sherman Tank. Source: Wikipedia.

Though we were two little devils, on Sunday our mothers *sent* us to church. My parents went to church only for funerals and weddings. Mother talked a better religion than she walked. They even stayed away at Christmas and Easter. As an adult, Patti was my sponsor when at age twenty-five, after having had six children, and after Charles died—I made my Confirmation at the Blessed Sacrament Cathedral in Detroit.

I do not recall that Charles or his family ever attended church. My grandmother, Sena Catherine Blagg, took my brothers and me from the time I was five.

Patti was also in my wedding party. She and her husband are my children's godparents. We were all raised in the same neighborhood.

I attended the local school, Erin Elementary; Charles and my brothers attended East Detroit Junior High and East Detroit High School. Charles didn't finish school in Michigan. Shortly after he was sixteen, he moved to Chicago. He was nineteen when he returned to Detroit, having graduated high school in Chicago. His parents had moved back to Detroit and his father had resumed work at Dodge Main, the company's primary factory location.

By this time, my parents had moved and we were living a block from the Bennetts. I was nearly sixteen and working after school at Cunningham's Drugstore. I was in the eleventh grade and an art major (costume illustration, dress design, and sewing). I also took extra classes in mathematics and sciences.

I was studying art only to please Mother. I thought that perhaps by pleasing Mother, we could get along better. In truth, what I wanted to do was join the Army and train to be a nurse. It never happened. I became a nurse after

Charles was killed. However, not all was lost. I am a good dress and costume designer; I can create patterns and sew many items. I made all the costumes for my children at school. The quality of my work was good; it was exempted from school contests as unfair.

Charles and I started dating the year he returned from Chicago. We became engaged sometime just before my seventeenth birthday. In today's vernacular, my *Art-Carved* engagement ring was "to die for." Sadly, it was in the house when the explosion happened. I lost it. Why didn't I wear it? It was beautiful, but not practical. Charles had paid $500 for the ring in 1950. It was elegant.

My engagement picture was horrible, because of the dress that had been given to me by my Mother. It was a navy-blue dress with large polka dots, a bouffant skirt, and shoulders designed for a Detroit Lions football player. I am five feet tall; then I weighed ninety-five pounds. The dress dwarfed me. It fit, but it was such a sight that it removed the focus from the bride-to-be and put it squarely on the dress itself. I had to wear it—there was no polite way to avoid it.

***

When we returned, Charles went to work at the Dodge Motor Company in Detroit. He was twenty, working on the assembly line. He must have had a fair wage, as he always had plenty of money.

I went to work at *Sears* as a salesclerk. We moved into a one-room apartment in Detroit, a short bus ride to the Dodge Main plant or to the *Sears* store at Van Dyke and Gratiot. We had a kitchenette but shared the bathroom with another tenant.

Later we moved into one of the apartments in Mother's apartment building, further away from work, but since I was pregnant, it was a problem only for Charles. It was still a one-ride bus trip. We knew that the one-room would be too small once the baby arrived. She told us the apartment was available, and we grabbed it. Again, it was to please my mother in a developing love/hate relationship. We were living there when Jocey was born.

Chapter 6: The Arrangements

Very little in the house was salvageable, yet looters were busy trying to find treasure to remove. During the mid-morning on the day of the explosion, the police department called Mother's house, asking if a family member could go to the house to board-up windows and doors. She called my brother Louis and asked him to go. Fred and his wife had taken my father to the hospital.

Not knowing if the police would still be at the house, he took a pistol with him. A police officer awaited him. The house was full of people just wandering around. Aware that the police officer was powerless to force them to leave, nobody had paid attention to the officer. Louis entered the living room, pulled out the pistol, and yelled, "I have a pistol, and I'm an expert shot. You have ten seconds to leave my sister's house or I'll start shooting." In a few minutes, the officer and Louis were busy nailing boards over the blown-out windows and nailing the doors shut.

These people were not the neighbors. When my brother arrived at the house, he had difficulty finding a parking space; when he left, there were many to be had. He would later tell me that photographers had been there—no doubt the newspapers and television stations, perhaps one or more fire investigators, and certainly some curiosity seekers. In those days, black and white pictures needed flashbulbs for interior shots, and the property was littered with them.

***

Charles had been moved to the morgue. There was a coroner's inquest on the following day, December 26. On the 27th, my mother got a call from the Detroit Morgue that the body could be picked up because an autopsy was not required. Fred had to identify him a second time before the body could be transferred from the morgue to the funeral home: *Reed-Shultz* on Gratiot Avenue in East Detroit, where the casket was open for viewing.

While it was open, a beautiful rose-colored veil was placed over the open portion of the casket to prevent anyone from touching his body. His hands were at his sides; too badly burned to be crossed over his chest, as is the custom. The rose blanket that would have gone over the lower half of the casket was displayed on a small table place directly in front of the casket to prevent people from getting too close. Whoever embalmed his body had done a very good job, considering the condition of the body.

One of Charles' cousins brought his young daughter to the viewing. With the tactlessness of a young child, she looked at the casket and asked, "Why is there a big doll in that pretty box?" When I heard her, I became angry enough to toss them both onto the street. The adult must share the blame for the comment because he failed to prepare the little girl. I still become angry when I recall how hurt I was by that little girl's statement that night so long ago. I must learn to forgive. I must.

There were two days of visitation. Charles had only recently entered the process to convert to Catholicism, so a local Baptist minister officiated. There was no official wake. However, we were at the funeral home from ten a.m. to ten p.m. on each of the two days before the burial. I was grateful that a priest and several nuns were at the funeral.

On December 30 at 1:30 p.m., Charles was buried in Forest Lawn Cemetery on Van Dyke Street and Six Mile

Road in Detroit. I decided the only way to get through it was not to think about the future. I was focused on the moment.

***

As the days passed after the funeral, I began to be angry at everything. It became harder and harder to conceal the rage. I hated my life. I hated even being born. I hated having married Charles. I hated having the children. I hated having bought the house. I hated the realtor for hiring unskilled laborers to work on my house. I hated myself because if I hadn't married and had children, none would be hurt.

Everything turned into stress. I wished people would just go away. Rage worked its way out of my body at times, such as when I would shower and beat the sides of the shower stall with my fists. Moreover, I found that I was impervious to the pain. Other times, to handle the rage, I would walk several miles around Detroit until I was too exhausted to care. Later, when I applied for work at the Children's Hospital, I found that being there only increased my rage; I told them I wasn't interested.

As military personnel are told to do when facing insurmountable problems, I suppressed my anger and got on with what I had to do. Slowly I became dead to the pain. It's been sixty-five years now, and the suppressed rage is still there. In a way, composing this book has become a catharsis, and while others have certainly experienced and written about PTSD, I'm hopeful that my perspectives and the things I experienced will give another sufferer hope.

Several especially pertinent incidents occurred between the morning of the explosion and the days following.

On December 27, when Fred went to the morgue for the second identification of Charles' body so it might be released to the funeral home in East Detroit, a reporter was waiting to interview him. A large man not to be trifled with, Fred demanded that the reporter leave. The arrangement at the funeral home allowed viewing through a large window at the top of a flight of stairs. A gurney containing the body was placed close to the window. As the curtain opened so Charles' body could be viewed, a flashbulb ignited. Fred turned quickly around and decked the reporter with a fist firmly planted to the jaw.

The reporter hit the floor and his camera went tumbling down the long flight of stairs. The man was on his feet in seconds. The attendant came from the viewing room and looked at the reporter to see if he had been hurt. When he saw that the man's pride and his camera were the only things damaged, he suggested that the reporter be more careful when climbing stairs; he could get hurt.

After the reporter left, the curtain was again opened and Fred identified Charles from a malformed index finger on his right hand. An autopsy had not been done because at the inquest it had been determined that the cause of death was a furnace explosion.

Another incident occurred at the funeral home: the owner of the realty company came to the funeral home on the evening of the inquest at the local fire department and sat down beside me. He'd return the down payment I had given his company when we purchased the house in October, he said. It was an act of God but he wanted to do something to help. Just that morning I'd been told that the reason the explosion had occurred was that his unlicensed worker had failed to put a safety valve on the furnace. Yet here the realtor was, attempting to blame God. In truth, the realtor stood to be liable for the explosion, and he was attempting to buy my silence. I refused the money. Thirty years later, Scotty and Shirley were each able to exact a financial settlement from the realtor.

I was alone in the funeral home, sitting in the room with my husband's casket. The rest of my family and friends had not yet arrived. Mr. Reed, of the funeral home, must have heard the front door open when the realtor came in. I didn't see him in the room until he was standing in front of us. Mr. Reed angrily told the man to leave the building and to stay out. He told him that should he make further attempts to speak to me again the funeral he would have him arrested for trespassing.

Finally, I had a friend besides the firefighter, the doctors, my lifelong friend Patti, and my dad. Patti and her husband were the first people to arrive at the funeral home. My closest friend was gone but just maybe others understood and would not try to be me, not try to tell me they knew just how I felt. People could not possibly know how I felt nor could they know how I was viewing the world. Had they, in the past, had their souls ripped-out?

Then, with the possibility that I might also lose Scotty and Shirley, there was absolutely no way they could ever have an idea about how I felt.

I was numb. Very quickly I trained myself to block some of my thoughts—the ones too painful to consider. *Don't think any further ahead than necessary,* I told myself. *Don't worry about tomorrow. It will take care of itself. Your children are depending on you. Nobody out there is concerned about you. So suck it up and go on. You're strong. You can do it.*

Sometime later I overheard my mother tell one of her friends that if a tragedy of such proportions had to happen in her family she was glad that it happened to *my* husband and me and not to one of my brothers' family members, because they could never cope. Mother was an absolute gem.

When Fred returned to mother's house, my father asked about the other children. Without thinking, Fred stupidly said, "There are only these two," implying that my other four children and I had also died in the explosion. Before Fred had a chance to correct himself, my father went into shock. Fred now realized my father's situation he and his wife Estelle took Daddy to Saratoga Hospital. Along the way, Fred tried to correct what he'd said to his father, but Daddy was too far-gone into shock.

He would spend the next few days hooked up to intravenous tubes, grieving intensely. Because of his age and how he had reacted to the tragedy, he was hospitalized until after the funeral. No one could convince Daddy that I wasn't dead. He wouldn't eat. Mother somehow saw this as her *shining moment* and visited neither her gravely ill spouse nor her seriously injured grandchildren. She assumed she'd be getting the kids, and that made her intensely happy. Fred has never shown remorse for this action, and by the time he'd realized his mistake, he was unable to communicate with his father. I find it interesting that I can forgive my mother while being unable to forgive the little girl with the insensitive question.

Three days later when I left the hospital to arrange for Charles' funeral, I visited Daddy at Saratoga Hospital. When I entered his room, he started to cry. He would be ok; I was alive, so he could go on. Fred waited for me to finish at the funeral home and then returned me to the Children's Hospital. He then went to the morgue again to identify the body of my husband so the funeral director could ready the body for the wake.

We were not the only ones affected. The East Detroit Chief of Police lived across the street and was one of Charles' hunting buddies. He had suffered a heart attack late in November and had come home on Christmas Eve. The explosion sent him back into shock because of Charles' death and the injuries to the children. Back he went to Saratoga Hospital. He did survive, but Christmas Eve of 1958 was one that nobody on the block will ever forget.

***

On Christmas Eve, on the way home from Mother's, we'd passed the *Reed-Shultz Funeral Home*. I noticed that the building was full, judging from the parking lot. My heart and a prayer went out to the people who experienced such grief at Christmastime. Never could I have imagined that in a few all too short hours I'd be there.

Many people want to know the future. I don't. I don't want to remember the past either but at times for no reason I have vivid, clear flashbacks. It has taken me more than sixty years to realize that if you want to experience love and be able to laugh at yourself, you must also be capable of feeling pain.

Anger and hatred are still large parts of my life but most of the time I am in control. In many ways, I still experience the shock. Perhaps this book will return some order to my life. Most of the time, I am happy with myself. I still have difficulty at times knowing when it is acceptable to feel pain and when I need to hide it away in my special place.

I was not on the best of terms with my mother. I could tell much about her, but I choose not to speak ill of the dead. That's something I've learned with my PTSD. I may share my hurt in counseling, but this is my story, not hers. Except for an explanation of its effect on me, that's the way it will be.

The best illustration of this was what my brother told me she'd said when she first got the call about the explosion. She'd knocked on Fred's door and said, "Get up. That stupid idiot has burned down his house!" There was no love lost between Charles and his mother-in-law.

On my first visit to Mother's home, Jocey told me her grandmother had told her Charles was dead. Because Jocey was taking Catechism classes at St Veronica's school, she knew about death. When I heard that, I was furious. Whenever possible my mother would play the martyr. She had no right to tell Jocey about her father's death. She knew only what she'd heard from others. Others knew only what I had told them. I am sure Mother played a scene that would have made Sarah Bernhardt envious. Again, I steeled myself and went on.

Only Josey can remember Charles. Her only memory of her father—remember that she was age seven—was of a movie the two watched together three days before Christmas, 1958. It was the day he bought my Christmas present—a radio—which I found in my jeans the night of the disaster. On the movie night, the snow was so deep that Charles carried her home on his shoulders from the nearby movie house to which they had walked. It was four years before she could remember the name of the movie they saw. It was *Tales of the Crypt.* Jocey liked horror stories.

Chapter 7: Following Release

Jocey was the first to be released. Of the three, her burns were the least significant, and she had made tremendous progress. She would have only one follow-up visit and her treatment would be finished. My father picked her up at the hospital

Shirley would remain in the Children's Hospital for three months. Her burns had been quite severe. Unfortunately, that wasn't the end of it. She had as many as three operations a year until she was twenty-one, for longstanding damages to her face, leg, and heel and the need to adjust for her growth. Her face and right heel needed the most work. The surgeries were performed at University of Michigan Children's Hospital.

Scotty stayed the longest in the Children's Hospital Of Michigan, Detroit. Once he was put on a ward, he began physical therapy. He would need to stretch the newly grafted skin and tone the muscles in legs that hadn't been used in several months. He needed help with balance and spent time on the parallel bars there in the therapy room. It took a while before he could stand on his feet without assistance. No longer attached to the *Stryker* frame, he spent most of his time either in a wheelchair on in bed. Part of his therapy was tub soaks, and that continued even after he was discharged in May of 1959.

Two small children who were burn victims were next door to the room that held Jason and Sharon. They had each been hospitalized for a month or so when my children were admitted. One of the children was younger than two years. His feet had been burned so severely that the toes on one foot had been amputated. His mother had put him feet first into the tub for a bath. The water was too hot. In 1958, physicians were not required to report suspected child abuse cases to the authorities.

The other little boy was ten months old when he rolled off the daybed and his head was wedged between the radiator and the bed. It was winter and the metal was hot. His mother was vacuuming and didn't hear him crying out in pain. He lost his ear before his mother had discovered him. I never saw their father visiting and the mothers rarely were there and stayed only for short visits when they did come to the hospital. The physicians were still doing reconstruction on them when Shirley was discharged. Donald and the older boy spent a couple of months together in the ward after Donald was moved from isolation. He relearned to walk while we were there. We often played together.

***

My world was beginning to unravel. The first real evidence of it came one afternoon while Scotty was in therapy. I'd gone for a walk. The morning was exquisite. The walk regenerated my spirit and I stayed away from the hospital for more than an hour. Scotty was still in therapy when I returned, so I decided to join him. That was a big mistake.

As I neared the room, I heard both Scotty and the therapist laughing. That was a good sign, so I quickly popped into the room, refreshed and a smile on my face, which turned ashen rather quickly. I was unprepared for what I saw. Never having been to one of these sessions, I didn't know what to expect. Scotty was walking on a sterile sheet that had been placed between the parallel bars.

Blood was oozing from the dressings on his legs. It ran down his legs and onto the sheet. I immediately became dizzy.

The therapist tried to waive me out of the room before Scotty and I made a visual connection. I backed out of the room and up against a wall, slid down the wall, and sat on the floor with my knees against my chin until someone came to rescue me. I never returned to any of his therapy sessions. I'm not a squeamish person: I'd seen blood before and after. But this was *my* kid who'd been hurt, and I couldn't stomach what he had to go through. That experience commissioned a new set of recurring nightmares. I was developing an extensive catalog of frightening nights.

Across the hall from Scotty's ward, in a private room, was a small boy, sick with terminal cancer. When he could, this boy would come into the ward and talk to Scotty and the other boys. After a couple of weeks, he didn't come out of his room again. He was too weak. He died a few days later. When I explained to my son why the little boy would never again come to talk, Scotty asked if the little boy was in Heaven. Then he asked if he would be going to Heaven soon to be with Daddy and the little boy? I assured him that he would be staying with his family for many years to come. The little boy was never mentioned again, but Scotty had learned when people die they never return to earth but that we may someday go to be with them.

Physical pain and sorrow had become the normal way of life for both of us regardless of how hard I tried to protect him. Though nearly everything that had happened to the children and me since Christmas morning had been out of my control, I still blamed myself. It was irrational, yes, but despair became my alter ego. I didn't realize just how many years I'd suffer from this despair. As I write these words—even though I realize intellectually this is nearly sixty years ago—I am heavily affected emotionally.

Scotty came home from the hospital in May on the Friday before Mother's Day. It was wonderful to see him walk unaided from the car to my mother's house. The doctors had told me before he left the hospital that he would need to continue physical therapy. We returned to Detroit daily for nearly two months. In addition, they suggested I get a pony for Scotty to ride daily. Sitting on the pony to ride would help his legs, they said, in a way that no amount of therapy could accomplish. We went, all seven of us, to find a pony.[10]

We found a pony whose name was Jim, and he was delivered to my mother. All the kids loved their new friend. Scotty became a great horseman. Today horses are used

---

[10] Equine-Assisted Psychotherapy uses the horse as a tool for a licensed therapist to provide mental health treatment. Young people who ordinarily shun physical and emotional closeness with other people can often accept it from a horse. The bond between child and horse can help children develop trust, respect, affection, empathy, unconditional acceptance, confidence, responsibility, assertiveness, communication skills, and self-control. To succeed with a horse, children must exercise patience, understanding, attention, forgiveness, and consistency—abilities they will find useful throughout their lives.

for many people who need help walking and balancing. Similar activities exist around the country.[11]

Scotty returned to the Children's Hospital twice for surgery during the year following the explosion. After those two operations and six office visits, he never returned. When he had his last operation, one of his front teeth was loose. When he was returned to his bed in the former Polio Ward after the surgery, the tooth was taped to his chart. The Doctor removed it from the chart and put it under his pillow. The tooth fairy comes in all sizes, shapes, and professions. Thank God for tooth fairies who can put broken little boys back together.

***

Several things affected Scotty's recovery after he was released from Children's Hospital. He'd had been home from the hospital for only a few days when I received a call from the administrator of the hospital. She asked if I would allow Scotty to attend four fundraising dinners. The hospital had always been funded privately. In the spring of 1959, the Children's Hospital was near closure. Not a publicly funded hospital, its elderly benefactors were dying, and most had not remembered the hospital in their wills. The building was now seventy-five years old and

---

[11] Equine-Assisted Psychotherapy uses the horse as a tool for a licensed therapist to provide mental health treatment. Young people who ordinarily shun physical and emotional closeness with other people can often accept it from a horse. The bond between child and horse can help children develop trust, respect, affection, empathy, unconditional acceptance, confidence, responsibility, assertiveness, communication skills, and self-control. To succeed with a horse, children must exercise patience, understanding, attention, forgiveness, and consistency—abilities they will find useful throughout their lives. Source: Wikipedia.

needed repair. These donations had dwindled over the years.

All the hospital employees had voted for Scotty to represent what could be done to save and restore children to normal lives by the doctors, nurses, and everyone at the hospital. He would be accompanied by a doctor and his hospital therapist. He would not be alone at any time and would be their poster child.

The hospital began a fundraising effort. As a part of this effort, the hospital applied to the Red Feather organization for a grant. *Red Feather* was the original name of the *Community Chest Fund*, what we today call the *United Fund*.

They knew they had only one chance to present their best face. They decided that Scotty could demonstrate the impact of a Detroit without a children's hospital. He was evidence of the skills and capabilities of the hospital, so he was named *Mr. Children's Hospital* in the spring of 1959. I dressed him in a little suit and they put a sash from shoulder to waist. The campaign was quite successful. The hospital still exists, going strong sixty years later. The hospital has never since been underfunded. Detroit Children's Hospital is today one of the Shriner's Hospitals for Children.

The second was sad. A year after Scotty's accident, on Christmas Eve of 1959, Jason's favorite nurse was murdered. She was robbed and killed just a few steps from the door of Children's Hospital. She was on her way to work. Scotty and I read about the murder in the paper on Christmas Day of 1959. He reacted to it very badly. We sent flowers, but we didn't attend the funeral. I'd decided that the only funerals we would attend would be for family.

The third made me angry. During the summer of 1959, Scotty and I were riding a bus on our way to the hospital. On the bus, we were accosted by a man who began to chastise Scotty about his burns, saying that the accident wouldn't have happened had he not been playing with matches. I tried to explain to the man what had happened and asked him to shut up—his father had died in the explosion. He continued to rant, rather more loudly.

The people around us were becoming uncomfortable. Unwilling to fight with the man in public, I dropped my head and averted eye contact. I had all my kids to protect. Shortly, the bus driver stopped the bus, told the man to shut up and get off the bus, and escorted him to the door, advising him never to take the bus again. The idiot exited the bus, still shouting his "advice." The memory of it still affects me. I periodically relive the altercation.

Following Charles' death and the kids' hospitalization, I continued to operate in a subdued fashion. I wasn't in a trance; I could function—but barely. I began to do erratic things. For example, I received the contents of Charles' pockets in a manila envelope from the Police. He had some Christmas tree hangers that he'd apparently bought on the way home from work. There was a comb and a billfold with his identification and twenty dollars in cash—his "mad money." I kept the money for a very long time, refusing to spend it. I kept his clothes and shoes in the closet of my home, as if somehow the existence of his apparel put him there with me. Ultimately, they became moldy and I discarded them.

For the next twenty years, while the children enjoyed the season, Christmas didn't exist for me. I always ensured that the kids had memorable holidays. As for myself, I always made sure that I worked on Christmas Eve and Christmas Day. If I were invited to someone's party, I always had a built-in excuse—I had to work. God had taken my Charles on Christmas—His Son's birthday. I wasn't prepared to forgive God for that, though the Christian side of me knows better. Christmas was "Hell" to me. While the kids were home, we celebrated—or rather, they celebrated, and I sat back and watched, trying to forget, fighting the choking tears. They understood, of course, but being children, Christmas was special to them. They were healing. I never have. Because we were living in my mother's home, I put on a show for her. I had to. I played the game. I moved from Mother's home the next time in June of 1959.

Once the kids were gone, however, even after we had moved into another house, I made sure I was otherwise occupied during the Christmas season. I worked. I worked for other people. If Hanukkah were close, I double-shifted for my Jewish friends. Then I'd come home, eat, and stare at the wall. Or I'd sit in the living room with the television playing for background noise, while I ignored the programming in favor of reflective thinking.

This continued for years, during which time I steadfastly avoided mourning Charles—he'd be coming home any day now. Over the years, my brother David would be killed, and both my daughter Shirley and my father died, just eight days apart. I don't recall whether I avoided mourning or just simply didn't mourn. The reality of the accident didn't hit me until Christmas of 1990, and when it did, I had all I could do to handle it.

As early as 1972, I understood what was happening to me was long lasting. Scripture says, in Proverbs 14:1

"Every wise woman buildeth her house: but the foolish pulls it down with her own hands." (KJV) Do I suffer from PTSD or am I just foolish? How many times since 1972 have I debated this with myself? My answer—I suffer from PTSD. Several times since, I have awakened from sleep in a state of panic. Mother, by the way, died in May of 1976. It took that long for me to forgive her, and you haven't yet heard about many of her actions.

***

When people are injured as seriously as my children were, occasionally in later years they develop Diabetes. By the time Shirley was sixteen she had it. She controlled it by diet most of the time. She died at twenty-five when she began to have trouble controlling her sugar.

Shirley had her last reconstructive operation at the University of Michigan Mott's Children's Hospital at twenty-one. She was in a very bad marriage. Six months before she died, she'd returned to her husband, who was physically controlling and verbally abusive. The daily stress for a Diabetic was too much. On January 4, 1981, she had a snack in the evening and sometime later, she fainted, aspirated, and suffocated. Her husband found her dead about two hours later when he returned home. She left behind two little boys. Eight days later my father, for whom I had been caring, died. Daddy was in his nineties. He'd been in my care for seventeen months.

Scotty was the last to be released from the hospital. At the time, we were all staying at my mother's house. As soon as I had time and with Charles' insurance money, I went looking at new houses. I found one almost at once. It was a three-bedroom brick house with a basement. The basement had a half bath. It would not be ready, I was told, for another two months. I bought it and started to replace what we had lost in the explosion. The house was not ready on time. The painters went on strike before the interior of the house was complete. We moved in just before school started in the fall.

Shirley, Scotty, and I were kept busy traveling from one hospital or the other with office calls tucked in between the surgeries during the summer of 1959. Both of Scotty's final two operations were complete and he was finished with therapy before classes started in September. Shirley had one hospital stay at the University of Michigan's Mott's Children's Hospital before we were in the house. Our new home was in Roseville, about one and a half miles from the house on Evergreen.

The nightmares started almost at once after we settled in the new place. I did not know I was screaming-out in my sleep. Jocey told my father about it. She didn't tell my mother because of the strained relationship between Mother and me. Daddy would last only another six months.

A short time after we moved into the new place my father started coming over nightly after the kids were in bed. One time I woke-up in my father's arms, crying. I must have been sleepwalking, as well, as we were standing in the kitchen.

Jocey had told my father I woke her every night with my screams. It was nearly fifteen years before the screaming stopped but the dreams didn't, although they became fewer and fewer over time. Even now, the dreams of Charles occasionally return. In these dreams, I don't see his face. I picture him behind me, but I recognize his voice. The dreams have changed. Today they are peaceful, not frightening—most of the time. But they are still there. Charles still comes to me, even after 65 years!

After the children who were old enough to attend school were settled into their classes and I had arranged for sitters, I returned to work. I went to work at a now-defunct hospital in Detroit called Marten Place Hospital. Marten bankrupted in 1970.

In Chapter 9, I will relate an experience that resulted in my winning an automobile. Before then, I had traded the car and purchased a station wagon. It had more room. I drove every morning to work after the kids were off to school. I was habitually late. I was in the OR, so I could manage the tardiness. I was the one who made out the surgery schedules, so I could pace myself and arrive in time to help set up the rooms and be sterile in time to assist the surgeon assigned to me by my supervisor.

It was a great place to work—until my mother started calling. Mother was suffocating me and pressuring me to give up my children. She was on a power trip, and I was her target. Soon I discovered that at work I could forget about my problems. I laughed and joked with my co-workers. At work, I was continuously busy. No one there ever knew the real me. I loved the children but I hated going home.

After work, I had to face the fact that my life was changed forever. I had no one to talk to about what was truly bothering me. My best friend Patti had her own marriage and children to care for. I couldn't add my problems of everyday life to hers. She wouldn't have known what to say if I had told her what my life was like. How could anyone know? I began to withdraw myself from everyone but the children. So I worked, cared for the children, and slept sitting up in a chair or stretched out on the floor.

Only when I was in bed at night did I scream. One night, as I was sleeping on the floor of the living room, Cathy came running from her bedroom into the living room and out the front door. I ran after her. When I caught up with her, she was asleep. After that, I had her sleep in my bed with me so I'd know if she got out of bed. As time went by, the screams subsided until they happened only every few weeks. They have never stopped.

Chapter 8: More Family Details

As I said before, I attended Erin Elementary School. When the family moved into downtown Detroit in 1947, I transferred to *St. Charles Catholic School*. Because of local unrest, Mother chose to put me in parochial school. After that, I attended *Cass*. I finished high school in May of 1950, turned seventeen in July, and was married on August 7 of that year.

When I was twelve, my family was offered a good price for the farm and sold it. Dad was a "gentleman farmer," and Mother was happy to be there until her mother died. After that, we moved twice—first to Garfield Street in East Detroit and then into Detroit itself. Back in Detroit, there were many places for a teenager to find work. I was usually at the top of my class, so working and studying was never a problem.

We were living there when Jocey was born. Before Scotty was born, we moved into a two-bedroom house in Detroit, close to Charles' work. Shortly after Scotty's birth, Charles went to work for General motors in Livonia, Michigan.

With Charles working at the new plant, we decided to move closer to his work. The City of Wayne is a small town a few miles from Willow Run. Cathy and Shirley were added to our family while we lived there.

The night Jason was born, the GM plant burned to the ground and Charles was out of work for about a month, until GM bought the Ford Transmission Plant in Willow Run, Michigan. [12]

We lived on unemployment compensation. I went back to work at Holy Cross Hospital in Detroit where I learned to be an EKG technician. In those days, the hospital did the training.

Charles was very loving to me. He was always overjoyed with the prospects of fatherhood. When I was pregnant with our first child, he gave me a beautiful orchid corsage for Mother's Day to wear to dinner and to my parents' home. Each year thereafter, I received a corsage from him as a Mother's Day gift.

Jocey was born on July 7 (our anniversary) at the Highland Park Osteopathic Hospital in Highland Park

---

[12] Located in suburban Detroit, the new Livonia plant was recognized as one of the most advanced manufacturing and assembly operations in the world. It had the capacity, tooling, and expertise in building planetary gear transmissions to fulfill market expectations for the boom times ahead. Four years later, errant sparks from a welder's tool touched off a firestorm that reduced the operation and its 3,318 machines to grotesque piles of twisted metal and charred bricks strewn across thirty-four acres of smoldering wreckage. At $50 million (almost $500 million in today's dollars) it was—and still is—the most destructive industrial fire in American history.

Livonia was the sole source of Hydra-Matics, turning out 4,000 per day. It had produced its four millionth unit prior to the Aug. 12, 1953, conflagration. Ninety percent of Oldsmobiles were equipped with the transmission, as were 85 percent of Pontiacs and all Cadillacs and Lincolns. The transmissions were also installed in some 50 percent of Hudson, Kaiser, and Nash vehicles. There were no customer backlogs; Hydra-Matics went into vehicles as soon as they were received.

Because of the fire, GM furloughed 26,000 employees, placed thousands more on reduced hours, and slashed new car production by 100,000 units. Suddenly, the world's largest company faced a monumental crisis.

Note that several of these automobiles no longer exist.

Source: https://www.assemblymag.com/articles/95000-americas-Most-destructive-industrial-fire.

Michigan. Four of our other children were also born there, a baby in each of the following four years.

At birth, Jocey weighed eight pounds and was a healthy baby. Her doting father and my mother named her. "Jocelyn" had been the name of Charles' sister who died at age eight from cancer. They differed on Jocey's middle name. Mother wanted her middle name to be Kaye (Kaye Starr was a singer who was popular in the fifties, and Mother was a fan). Mother won, but we did change to spelling to K-a-y. We took her home a few days later. Charles sat up all night watching her sleep. He couldn't have been happier. He acted the same with each child we brought home.

Shirley and Jason were our only children to remain in the hospital for a short time following their births. Shirley was born prematurely and remained in the hospital nursery for a few days after I was released. Jason was born with an obstruction, requiring surgery at Highland Park Hospital when he was twelve hours old. He was subsequently transferred by ambulance to Children's Hospital of Michigan, where he was on IVs for ten days. Fortunately, he responded to treatment quickly, though he lost weight. He was seven pounds, six ounces when he was born but was down to six pounds, ten ounces when we brought him home. He had to be taught how to drink from the baby bottle. He was not allowed an unsupervised bottle or a pacifier.

Scott Allen was born eleven months and three weeks following Jocey's birth on June 30, 1952, at 11:57 p.m. He weighed eight pounds, nine ounces. He was the best-behaved newborn of the family. We had to wake him for each feeding; else, he would sleep for ten hours at a time.

He was healthy and was never any trouble. His complained only when you tried to put him into a crib or playpen. One day my father brought a full size bed and mattress set to our house. The legs had been cut-off. When he put it together, the mattress was only off the floor by inches. We put thick fluffy rugs on the floor by the outer side of the bed and pushed the other side against the wall. Pillows were then placed around the edges of the mattress so he wouldn't roll off. Greta, my Doberman, slept on the floor beside Scotty whenever he was in bed. He was as safe as a child could be and slept much of the time.

Donald Hefka Bennett was another story altogether. Born on August 13, 1953, at 2:00 a.m., he was fourteen months younger than Scotty. He weighed eight pounds, eleven ounces. He was a fussy baby. He came into the world crying, cried all the way home from the hospital, and did not stop crying until he was nine months old. According to the doctor, he stopped crying then because he got tired of it.

Donny was a large child, beginning with nearly nine pounds of baby fat. His baby picture, taken at birth, was adorable. Of course, I'm biased. His face was so fat that his eyes were tightly closed. He looked like a puppy not yet ten days old. Although older, Scotty never did catch up to Donny's size. Today, Donny is six-feet-three-inches tall and has the nicest personality of any of my children. Scotty is five feet, ten inches.

When Donny was about nine months old, he started to bleed spontaneously from his nose. We took him to the closest ER where the on-duty physician packed his nose, sent us home, and advised us to follow up with our pediatrician. The boy was not in pain and was otherwise healthy. These bouts of bleeding from his nose and easy bruising have continued. Donny and I were each diagnosed with Von Willebrand Disease. Von Willebrand disease (VWD) is the most common inherited bleeding disorder of both man and animals. It is caused by a deficiency in a protein needed to help produce platelets (a blood cell used in clotting) that seal broken blood vessels. The deficient protein is called Von Willebrand factor antigen.

When I was at the hospital one evening while in training (I later gained training as a nurse), I bled spontaneously from my esophagus. There wasn't much blood but since I'd had nosebleeds nearly all my life, as did my mother and son, I was hospitalized. Donny was seventeen. We both had a battery of tests. Von Willebrand is akin to hemophilia. The problem differs in that hemophilia can be passed-on by the mother only to her sons. Von Willebrand can be passed on to her children of either sex.

There are elements of the immune system known as *factors*. Factors 8 and 9 contain proteins that differ between this disease and hemophilia. It is fortunate that we have Von Willebrand instead of hemophilia because the latter is much harder to control. Control in both involves the transfusion of blood: I have had twenty-five units in my lifetime. Since Donny has never had to have an operation, he has not needed blood replacement.

Cathy was the last of our children born in the Highland Park Osteopathic Hospital. She also was the last natural birth that I had. Because of kidney problems, the rest of my children were born by Cesarean Section.

On October 25, 1954, Cathy was born. She was seven pounds, twelve ounces, and healthy. She had few problems growing up, until the fateful morning of Christmas Day,

1958. She was always a good student although she did repeat the first grade, when her teacher thought it would give her a better start in school. She had been through a lot for a little girl just four when she was burned.

Today she is fine. She travels throughout the country opening stores for a large retail chain. Her first husband was killed in an auto accident on Father's Day before Sally, Cathy's daughter, was born. Her first daughter was born in 1979 at Mt. Clemons, MI, on Cathy's eighteenth birthday. Coincidentally, my brother David was murdered on the same day in the office of his trucking company office on the west side of Detroit, the result of a suspected—but never proved—contract hit by the Detroit Mafia.

Five years later Cathy remarried, and with this man she had a second child—a girl named Debrah. The marriage lasted only a short time. She divorced him when Deborah was in kindergarten and she never remarried, raising her daughters alone. Cathy gave herself a trip to Europe for her fortieth birthday. She'd always wanted to spend a night in a castle. After the trip, she told me about her night in the first castle, in Germany. It had not been modernized. There was no central heating and she said she nearly froze to death. The next night she slept soundly. The second castle had central heating, not just fireplaces.

Shirley Louise was our fifth child. She was born October 4, 1955, at the Garden Place Hospital in Garden City, Michigan. I went into the hospital the night before the scheduled C-Section. The next morning the operation was delayed until the blood was delivered from the Red Cross Blood Bank in Detroit. Immediately after her birth, she was transferred from the operating room to the sick baby nursery and placed in an incubator.

A premature baby, she had the usual problems because of underdeveloped lungs. Each day after work, Charles would go to the hospital to see her. She was tiny. Her birth weight was four pounds, six ounces but she lost the six ounces in a day. After a week, she could manage on normal room air. A few days later, we brought her home.

When I took her into the doctor's office for a checkup, I had dressed her in a pretty dress and booties and a small ribbon in her hair. The doctor took one look at her and told me when I got home with her to put her into a nightgown so she could be comfortable. He said if I wanted a doll to go to a store and buy one. I suppose he was correct. I was just so happy she was okay that I'd gone overboard.

Jason Paul was born February 20, 1958 (ten months to the day before his dad was killed), at Highland Park Hospital in Highland Park, Michigan, at nine in the morning. The OB/GYN surgeon waited until his brother Scotty had come from surgery. Scotty had gone into the operating suite that morning to have an inguinal hernia repair. The doctors wanted me to know the outcome of his surgery before I had the C-Section.

Scotty, Jason, and I were all fine after our operations. It wasn't until the nursery room nurse tried to give water to Jason that we knew he was in trouble. He had projectile vomiting when he tried to swallow the water because nothing could reach the stomach. Surgery was performed when the surgeon was able to get to the hospital. Jason was a normal child after he learned to drink from the bottle. Later his only problem was with his teeth, which had been damaged by daily oral iron supplements taken until he was four. By the time he was twelve he was having root canals. He was in his late thirties when he needed a full set of dentures.

There is more to my immediate family, and they will be introduced at the appropriate time.

Chapter 9: Enter the Queen

On the day after New Year's Day, 1959, my mother received a call from an officer at the State Police barracks closest to her house. Could he speak with Denise, he asked. She told the officer I was at the hospital with the children.

The show opened with host Jack Bailey. On the air, he said that the State Police officers had arranged for two tickets to the *Queen for a Day* television show at The Music Hall in Detroit [13] on January 9, 1959. Bailey asked the audience—mostly women— "Would YOU like to be Queen for a day?" After this, the contestants were introduced and interviewed, one at a time, with commercials and fashion commentary interspersed in between. Each contestant was asked to talk about the recent financial and emotional hard times she had experienced. The interview would climax with Bailey asking the contestant what she needed most and why she wanted to win the title of *Queen for a Day*. Often the request was for medical care or therapeutic equipment to help a chronically ill child, or might be for a hearing aid, a new washing machine, or a refrigerator.

---

[13] *Queen for a Day* was an American radio and television game show that helped to usher in American listeners' and viewers' fascination with big-prize giveaway shows. *Queen for a Day* originated on the Mutual Radio Network on April 30, 1945, in New York City before moving to Los Angeles a few months later and ran until 1957. The show then ran on NBC Television from 1956 to 1960 and on ABC Television from 1960 to 1964. Source: Wikipedia.

Many women broke down sobbing as they described their plights.

The winning contestant was selected by the audience using an applause meter; the harsher the contestant's situation, the likelier the studio audience was to ring the applause meter's highest level. The winner, to the musical accompaniment of *Pomp and Circumstance*, would be draped in a sable-trimmed red velvet robe, given a glittering jeweled crown to wear, placed on a velvet-upholstered throne, and handed a dozen long-stemmed roses to hold while her list of prizes was announced.

The prizes began with the help the woman had requested, and included a variety of extras, many of which were donated by sponsoring companies, such as a vacation trip, a night on the town with her husband, silver-plated flatware, an array of kitchen appliances, or a selection of fashion clothing. The losing contestants were each given smaller prizes.

Bailey's trademark sign-off was, "This is Jack Bailey, wishing we could make *every* woman a queen, for every single day!"

NBC picked up the show for national broadcast from January 3, 1956, to September 2, 1960

***

Someone would bring the tickets that day to mother's house, he said, if she were going to be at home all day. He couldn't give a time to her because of the nature of their work, but the dispatcher would call when the officer was on the way.

Mother called to tell about the tickets. I asked her to call the State Police back and thank them for their efforts, but I was declining because I didn't want to be away from the children. My children were too ill for me to leave them. "Don't accept the tickets," I told her.

Later, she called back. The officer had insisted that she take the tickets. He wanted no excuses. Again, I told her I wasn't leaving the kids for any stupid television show. Mother once again called the State Police and again told them I'd refused the tickets. The officer's answer was, "Tell your daughter that we will bring the tickets to her at the hospital and she will be accompanied to the Music Hall by the State Police officer who brings the tickets, unless she can provide her own transportation or go with a friend."

And they did. My best friend Patti and I went to the show. The officer had told my mother that the department had given all the money to my family that they could afford but that they were sure I would win. I could certainly use every prize I'd receive.

I do not know if *the fix* was in, but I did indeed win many prizes. Among them would be a trip to Hawaii. That trip would occur later in the year; after I was assured that my children were out of danger. I was in Hawaii when it became the fiftieth state in the Union.

***

The show was on January 9, 1959. Patti and I had to be there an hour and a half before it started. The hospital and the private duty nurse had the phone number of the Music Hall in case I was needed. We drove there in Patti's car. From the hospital, it was about a ten-minute drive to the theater.

When I gave the tickets to the ticket taker at the door, he deposited the large tickets (about the size of a file card) into a large container along with every other ticket and returned the stub portions to me. Prior to the tickets being deposited into the box at the door, the audience had to write on them why they wanted to be *Queen for a Day*. I wrote:

"I need a new car. I have three children in Children's Hospital and I stay with them most of the time. Twice a week I go to my mother's to visit the other children who were not hospitalized. My mother's house is a half an hour drive from the hospital. My husband was killed in the explosion that injured the three others."

During the time, the producer and his staff were reading each card for the reasons people wanted to be the winner, there was a short stage show. Betty White and Jack Bailey[14] were on stage with several singers and dancers.

When the pre-show was over, the curtains were closed and the producer came on stage. He announced the names of the five women chosen to appear; I was one. Numb, I sat in my seat after my name was called. Patti excitedly yelled, "Get up there; you'll win for sure." I did not want to go. I was never a demonstrative person. To me, this was just like standing on the corner with a tin cup. Later, Jack Bailey told me that I hadn't been a good contestant—I'd not screamed.

I also didn't know half the City of East Detroit was watching the show that morning. At St. Veronica's Parochial School, where my kids attended Catechism and Charles was studying to convert, the nuns were at the convent for lunch when the show came on the television.

---

14   Jack Bailey died in February 1980, after crowning more than 5,000 "Queens for a Day" during twenty years. As of this writing, we still have Betty White with us.

They were all in the social hall around the TV set. I was told later that when I won, the Mother Superior jumped up and down waving her arms yelling, "Jesus, Mary, and Joseph, she's won!"

When the final decision was made and I was declared the winner, they put a red robe around my shoulders and ushered me to a large throne. As Jack Bailey was attempting to put the crown on my head, he realized it was too large for me, so during the commercials he put his arm around my shoulders and slid his hand up under the crown so it wouldn't drop down over my face. The rest of the time that I was on camera, he sat next to me. I was so short that my feet didn't touch the floor so the robe was draped around my legs and feet. I was given a very large bouquet of roses. Then the audience and I saw all the prizes I had won, announced one by one.

When the show was over, Patti was escorted backstage by one of the ushers. I was busy signing for all the gifts. My shoe size was given to someone who returned a short time later to say I would be receiving a check from the producer because the company that had donated the year's supply of shoes to the show didn't make size five. The check was large enough to cover seven pairs of shoes in my size. In addition, I received kitchen appliances, a dinette set with a gold crown in the center of the table, a year's supply of *Tide*, a year's supply of pantyhose, a carton of women's disposable razors, a service for six of sterling silverware, and enough *Cruisewear* for a ten-day trip by ship to Hawaii and back. Patti and I were also treated to a night on the town, riding in a pink Cadillac, with Jack Bailey, Betty White, and their producer.

When it was planting time for roses in Michigan, I was sent a bush of the same kind of rose I'd received the day of the show. In addition to what has already been mentioned I also received a washer and dryer, a motion picture projector and screen, a check for the purchase of a car of my choice, a ten-piece bedroom set, and a year's supply of everything that had been advertised that day on the show. And I got the car—a 1959 Ford. The best part was that it was tax-free.

When Patti and I finally were able to take the trip, I was given a check for $500 to spend aboard ship. We had a suite on the promenade deck of a ship that was the flagship of the *Cunard Cruise Lines*.

We flew to San Francisco and stayed at the *Sir Francis Drake Hotel*. Our tickets were waiting there. It was Holy Thursday (the day before Good Friday). We ate at the hotel and spent several hours sightseeing. The next morning we had to board ship at noon, so we went to church early. Patti wanted to stop before we went to church to get a bottle of booze to take aboard the ship. She handed the bottle to me to put into my coat pocket just as we started to climb the stairs of the church. The stairs were crowded and someone bumped my elbow as I was putting the bottle into my coat pocket. It fell and broke, spraying booze all over me. All through the service people stared at me. I wanted to throw Patti into the bay.

When we were aboard ship, we discovered iced Champagne waiting for us in the cabin. It was a suite of two baths, a bedroom with twin beds, and a small sitting room with a couple of portholes. It was glorious, like something from a movie. When we were passing beneath the Golden Gate Bridge, the water became very choppy.

While trying to ride the elevators, we swayed from side to side. I'm claustrophobic: I started to feel sick. I'd been on the lakes in Michigan many times, but this was different.

We were at sea for about three hours when it was announced that everybody should take a life jacket from their cabins and proceed to the main deck. We didn't wait for an elevator. We ran up the stairs and found our assigned lifeboat. I trembled with fear. Had I survived an explosion only to die in a lifeboat at sea?

I was later told that maritime law requires this drill without warning. We were five days at sea, which was what I needed, but I could have done without the lifeboat drill. The trip helped me to get away from everything, if only for a short time. It was a true gift from God.

I sat on the deck chairs for hours at a time. Patti left me alone during these times. The rest of the time was spent eating the most wonderful food, swimming, reading, and dancing with every officer of the crew. I'm told that it's the duty of the officers to dance with all the single women. Every night, there was dancing. Variety shows were held each afternoon. Card games went around the clock. On the last day of the trip, there was an outdoor barbecue.

The ship had three bars open twenty-two hours a day, but food and beverages were served in the cabins twenty-four hours a day. It also had a large well-stocked library and dozens of shops. Everything was charged to your room until the night before arrival in port. The charges were delivered to the correct rooms while the passengers were at dinner that night.

We were told to have our luggage open and ready for inspection by the immigration people before breakfast the following morning. I wouldn't want to be an officer and must look through all those dirty clothes. All cameras had to be open and free of film. If we had anything in the ship's safe, we were to get the items when we paid our bill at the purser's office after dinner.

Patti had a few bills to pay, and I had some, such as telegraph charges, that were not covered by the Queen for a Day prize. All jewelry was to be kept in our handbags along with any foreign bills and would be checked by customs when we docked. We had breakfast at 5 a.m. so the officers could complete their duties before we left the ship. I think I could have stayed aboard that ship for a lifetime if I'd had my children with me. Aboard ship, I didn't feel as if I had been cursed.

It was early in the day when we left the ship. We went straight to the hotel. We were staying at the *Royal Hawaiian.* This suite was the same quality as the one aboard ship. It was beautiful. We had our own balcony overlooking the ocean. Shortly after we checked in, a waiter brought us a tray of freshly diced pineapple and coconut and a large bouquet of native flowers, complements of the show. Just down the hall from us, we later discovered were the main cast members of the Arthur Godfrey TV show. As soon as we could change clothes we were into our swimsuits and out to the beach. After swimming for a while, I fell asleep on the sand. Patti forgot to wake me and I ended-up with a very painful sunburn, made even more painful by the tight-fitting evening dress I wore to dinner that night.

The first night we retired very early. We were exhausted. All the dancing, swimming, and general excitement of being in Hawaii, and the simple fact that we were doing all this by ourselves took its toll long before midnight. The next morning, we were up and down to breakfast at dawn. We rented a car and drove all day just enjoying the beautiful scenery. We stopped at an outdoor café for lunch and another for dinner and a couple of drinks. We returned to the hotel about ten that evening and ended our day with a long walk along the beach with our shoes in our hands.

The night sky was enchanting. When we returned to our room, the beds were turned down and more fresh flowers were in the room. The message light on the phone was blinking. Patti answered it, thinking there was a call from home. I froze in my tracks until I heard her say, "Thank you, yes tea would be nice before bed. Please make it a pot with cream only. Thank you so much. Good night." After the waiter left, we changed clothes and sat on the balcony for a couple of hours.

Patti avoided mentioning Charles, for which I was very thankful. Again, we spent another happy night. We attended many shows day and night during the next couple of days. To me it seemed like the town was one big party day and night. The luau was like nothing I had ever seen before and I had been to many large banquets back home. Nevertheless, this luau was the mother of all feasts.

Later that night we were walking along the beach before returning to the room when we met two sailors from the naval base. We overheard them talking about the last bus to the base had left an hour before. So nice women that we were, we offered to take them home. The base was only a few minutes' drive away. We asked them if they would like to have dinner with us the next evening at the hotel. They were at the hotel about six the next night. Dinner was wonderful as always. The sailors were fun to entertain and somehow we ended up showing them our room. They stayed until about two o'clock in the morning. We hadn't told them we were married. I still wasn't accustomed to thinking of myself as a widow. They took it rather nicely when after a few kisses we said that we were leaving the next day and had to board ship early in morning but we would still drive them to the base.

When Patti drove up to the guard shack, she waved at one of the guards who had stepped out of the shack and proceeded to drive down the lane inside the fence. Our sailors were in the backseat of the car as Navy jeeps and sailors with guns surrounded the car. The two "swabbies" in the back of our car looked as if they were going to faint. The guards ordered all of us out of the car. After the guards checked the passes of the two sailors, they dismissed the men. Patti and I were ordered into the guard shack. We had to show our ID and were asked why we hadn't stopped at the gate as the guard had told us. We hadn't heard him say anything to us but of course, we were all laughing and talking so we just waved and drove on through the gate. The guard in charge suggested that we had given our room numbers to the sailors and they had called for prostitutes. The guards wanted to know what we were doing with these sailors.

We told the guards to check with the hotel and see if we were registered. After that was confirmed, we were allowed to leave with a warning never to drive past a guard at a Naval station without identifying ourselves again or we could go to jail. All the way back to the hotel we laughed about what Patti's husband Phillip and my mother would say if they knew about tonight's adventures. We felt like "ladies of the night." Oh to be that young and naïve again.

The next morning we were back aboard ship. The deck hands gave leis to everyone with instructions to toss them in the water as the ship pulled away from the dock and if they returned to the boat if meant you would return to the island. Mine did not return and neither have I.

***

The return trip by ship was as wonderful as the trip to the islands. We ate, played cards, danced, drank, and watched the whales play in the water as they migrated to Alaska. They acted as if they were putting on a show just for us. The last night out, the captain announced that a storm was forecast and that he was going to outrun it. The only thing the passengers would notice would be a slight increase in speed as the ship got under speed. It was hardly noticeable. Of course, I was expecting the worst. We docked in LA earlier than expected. We had to go through customs because the ship had originally sailed from another country. The line was long and very slow.

I couldn't wait to get to the hotel to go back to bed. It was early afternoon when I awoke. Patti had been down in the lobby shopping while I slept. I had just finished dressing. I noticed she was very nervous. Going out for breakfast did nothing for her mood. I didn't want to pry but I had to know what was wrong. I knew she didn't like flying so I ask her if the idea of the flight home was upsetting her. At her suggestion, we went shopping and returned after dinner. We were in the room for only a few minutes when Patti ordered a fifth of scotch. In only a few minutes, she had downed a quarter of the bottle. I tried to get her to bed but she wanted to tag all the packages loaded with gifts we'd purchased for the kids and everyone else. She did not want to wait until the following morning.

I packed those items going to Patti's house and those going to my mother's in different boxes. We were having them shipped by rail to save money. Air was too costly. Patti wrote out the labels while I packed. It was late when we finished and we went to bed. I left a call for six the next morning. I was awake before the call came from the desk. Patti was still nervous and it began to worry me. As we started to board the plane, she popped a couple of pain pills into her mouth. When we were buckled into our seat and ready for take-off she told me what was bothering her. Phillip was to meet us at the airport in Detroit. She told me that he might be a bit upset with us because he had no idea that we would be gone nearly three weeks. She had told him we were going for the weekend. How she made him believe that I will never understand.

There was no jet service in this country in 1959. It took three weeks for our boxes of gifts to get to our houses because Patti had mixed up the addresses. She had her address on mine with mother's city and I don't recall how she addressed hers but it was not even close to being correct. But we didn't care. We'd had the time of our lives and that was all that truly mattered.

Chapter 10: Oh, Mother!

Before I brought Scotty home from the hospital, my brother Fred, and his wife Waynetta moved back from Florida and were staying with our parents. I'd spent the last few weeks before Scotty's discharge from the hospital looking for houses. I'd hoped to find an available house so the kids and I could move in before his discharge. I had been promised that the house I'd picked would be available when needed.

That didn't happen. The one I chose was incomplete; it would take about two weeks to finish, according to the contractor. I would still have time to move before Scotty came home. In the interim, I got an FHA mortgage, purchased what household items I needed, called the producers of the television show on which I had appeared in January and told them when the prizes could be delivered, and waited for the house to be finished. It *still* wasn't completed in time. Before the house could be finished, the painters went on strike. That delayed our move-in date by a couple of weeks. Scotty had to come home to my Mother's overcrowded house. He was discharged the Friday before Mother's Day in May. He had spent 140 days at Children's Hospital.

***

I was born in the Detroit area and had lived there all my life. Every employed family member had belonged to one union or another, including me, starting with my father at Ford Motor Co. At this time in my life, however, I was concerned only about my children having a home and not about painters getting a raise. I wanted *out* of my parent's house. I needed to get out of their house and so did the kids. Mother's ideas of raising children and mine had never been the same. To our general disagreements was added the treatments Scotty needed daily. He learned that his grandmother could be manipulated. Often he wanted to delay the soaking of his bandages. She would tell him he could wait. When I insisted they be done on time, my mother demonized me.

Mother felt a great need to control everything. For example, she told the other children that the pony, Jim, was just for Scotty. It was not. Of course, it was to help Scotty regain strength and balance but it was for all the kids to ride, including my niece Jill. Mother didn't tolerate my nightmares very well either. If the strike hadn't been settled when it was and the house finished, I'm sure I'd have rented an apartment until the house was done.

I cannot tell you how wonderful it was to wake up and know it was moving day. I had very little to take from my parent's home. I had spent the last week at Mother's house clearing out the attic. Clothes that had been donated to us but which didn't fit were given to one of the churches for those who could use them. We packed only the household items that I wanted.

Waynetta was a big help. We moved fifteen or more boxes as soon as the kids had eaten breakfast that morning. I made sure that Scotty, despite his injuries, did his part, ensuring that he could handle the tasks. It was important that he felt a part of the move. Nobody but nobody—my mother included—would make my son an invalid. I'd resolve that he *would not* be considered handicapped. His burns were healing nicely; his hands were sensitive; and he needed to strengthen his arms. But he *wanted* to help. Mother was driving him crazy by babying him.

He would be returning to school in the fall. He had to be treated like any other boy if he were to grow up emotionally strong. The scars on his hand were my only concern. Those I protected.

The vans carrying the prizes given by the TV show arrived early. When the drivers of the vans had finished placing the bedroom furniture, fridge, washer, dryer, and kitchen table, (white Formica top with a gold crown in the center and chairs with white seats and chrome legs), into each room, there was little left to do. I waited for the living room furniture and the boy's bunk beds to be delivered from one of the local stores, while the kids unloaded the boxes that had been placed in each bedroom.

The bedroom set I'd won on *Queen for a Day* was too large for my room. There were ten pieces. The girls got the extra nightstands and the chests. I'd had carpet installed before we moved. When the living room furniture, TV, and the bunk beds were finally in place, I sat in the living room for a long time and listened to the kids with their new toys. Only Scotty had anything left from that tragic holiday six months before—his cowboy boots and holster that the fireman had had refinished. It was like Christmas for the children. They were happy and not worried about the future. I was the terrified one. I missed Charles. That day was the closest I'd ever get to feel real Christmas joy again.

The first night in the new house on Barkman Street was long and exciting for the kids. As hard as they tried, they couldn't settle down to sleep until long after midnight. The next day we all slept until nearly 10:00 a.m. After breakfast, we went shopping for things we'd forgotten to purchase in the days before moving. We brought home groceries, garbage cans, and cleaning supplies, plus bikes for everyone but Jason. At fifteen months, he was much too young.

The last thing needing to be done at the house was to have a lawn put in and a fence installed, but first I had to order fill dirt. Those first few weeks were filled with phone calls, lawn care, hanging drapes, and doctors' visits for

Shirley and Scotty. I had little time to think about being alone. What time I had was occupied by recurring and terrifying nightmares. Those wouldn't go away for a very long time.

Scotty decided he would go with my brother Fred to get the fill dirt. Fred and the two older boys were gone most of the morning. When they returned, we unloaded the truck. What a mess the boys and I were. The pile of dirt stayed in the front yard until the next day. Scotty had worn soft gloves so his hands were unaffected by blisters. However, the two of them were so tired they slept until nearly noon. (I never was tired enough to sleep without waking several times, although I did sleep for longer periods when I fell asleep in a chair or on the floor in the living room.)

After breakfast, I called my brother and asked when he would be over to spread the dirt, which was part of the deal (he'd borrowed a thousand dollars of Charles' insurance settlement). [An aside: Fred had borrowed $1,000. He said he'd pay the balance in a few months. Those few months turned into twenty-six years. If the car I'd purchased when I was caring for our father hadn't stopped working, he'd have never paid the balance.]

Of course, he was too busy. Therefore, the job was left to the boys and me. At the end of the day, we had about half of the dirt spread over the yard. The next day the boys were not eager to continue. They sat on the porch for about a half an hour, and then disappeared. When they returned, they had five or six girls in tow. Scotty got out all the shovels that Fred had left behind and distributed them among the help. The girls ranged in age from about nine or ten to about twelve. Those little ones worked their hearts out, while my sons sat on the porch and handed out drinks. Jocey was so embarrassed. She wouldn't leave the house that weekend except to go to Mass. Personally, I thought it was funny. Nevertheless, I was concerned about my brother's influence on the boys—it was something Fred would do. Both still love their Uncle Fred. Jason is a different story all together. He has never liked him.

One day shortly after moving to Barkman Street, I was at the kitchen table having coffee. We were about seven miles from Selfridge Air Force Base. The Air Force at that time had just finished lengthening the runways to accommodate larger jet aircraft. As one of the jets flew over our house, it broke the sound barrier. By the time I realized what had happened, I was standing in the middle of the street. I was trembling, crying, and looking back at the house. To my troubled mind, the noise of the plane was another explosion. I returned to the porch and sat for a while, regaining composure before I could go inside.

I was becoming extremely vigilant. About the only thing different was that I no longer planned escape routes. I'd done that ever since Charles and I had married. The first time I had planned my way out of a building in case of a fire was on our honeymoon. I did that also on the first night of each new place we stayed thereafter until he was killed. Until the incident with the plane, I was not aware I'd stopped doing that. There was no longer a need—the fire had happened.

When school started that fall, my kids didn't need new clothes. Nearly everything they had was new. I still had three children at home with me when the older kids were in class at the nearest public school. I'd have had to drive them to Catholic school. Therefore, those old enough to attend first Holy Communion classes went to Sacred Heart on Saturdays. I drove them to class and back. Often, we waited for them or went shopping until it was time to pick them up. Jocey, being oldest, was the first to make her communion. I went to Hamtramck to the same place I had bought my wedding dress to purchase her dress. It was beautiful. It looked like a small wedding gown.

I would be returning to work as soon as Shirley had her first reconstructive surgery at Mott's Hospital in Ann Arbor at the University of Michigan. That happened in October. When she was home and after the surgeon said a babysitter could care for her, I went to work in the operating room at Marten Place Hospital in Detroit. I received on-the-job training, which was often done in 1959 if one showed the desire to learn. I was planning to go into nursing, so I wanted to learn as much as possible while the kids were still small. I was generally home by four-thirty p.m., so the sitter was needed for all day, because I left at seven in the morning.

There was a long string of sitters, perhaps five, in just a couple of years. The first one was let go when I came home one day and two-year-old Jason was nowhere to be seen. He'd been outside playing with the older kids. When I asked the sitter about him, she said she hadn't seen him for a couple of hours, the last time with his brothers. When I found him, he was indeed with Scotty and Donny and was just fine, no thanks to the sitter.

The second sitter was almost as neglectful. When I heard from the kids what was happening with Shirley, I called the sitter and told her she could finish the week but that I wouldn't need her after that coming Friday.

As always, the kids and I went out for dinner on Fridays. We'd go shopping and sometimes went to a show.

Whenever we went out on Friday night, it was my habit to strip the beds and throw the sheets into the washer. I'd put them into the dryer when we returned later. Then I would make the beds with sheets from the linen closet while the kids were preparing for bed. That night I did it as always before we left. After we returned, when I went to the closet to get clean bedding, I discovered that the sheets were gone: every one of them and the matching pillowcases. I called mother to ask if for some reason she'd taken them. When I found out it was not Mother, I was furious. I knew who had them. The following day the kids and I went shopping again. I could do nothing. Sheets don't have serial numbers that can be traced.

I don't remember all the reasons the others did not stay longer than six months. I do recall the reason the last sitter left. One day, I returned from work to find the kids were all at Mother's house. After the kids were home from school she'd stopped by and taken them with her. Again, I was furious. Daily stress was my constant companion. The sitter had just allowed her to trot off with them without calling me.

After that, I could not trust anyone to watch the kids while I worked. I arranged for someone to care for them away from home. The older children were picked up after school by someone and I picked them all up when I finished work. The school was made to understand that no one other than I or someone I had introduced to them was to take the children from school. I didn't learn until after the children were grown that it was then that Fred promised Mother he would get the courts to take my children and give them to her. Charles' prediction was beginning to come true. I was fighting a losing battle.

My screaming nightmares worsened. I wanted to run away with the children as far as I had money to take us. How could I deprive the kids of the only family besides me that they had? Their father's family didn't see them again for years. I never saw Charles' brothers after the funeral. I began to consider day and night how I could move all of us away from my mother and Fred, the only family I had. I loved them, but I hated and feared them at the same time. Had I gone to the probate court I might have gotten help. However, by now I was beginning not to trust anyone. Not even God.

One day I came from work to hear from the parking lot attendant that Fred had taken my car. He had told the attendant I knew he was coming to get it. I took a bus as far as I could, which was Eight Mile Road and Gratiot Avenue. Then I had to take a bus from there to Gratiot and Frazho Road. From that point, I had to walk a mile to my house. It took three hours to get home.

The woman who cared for my kids had to return them to their home because I still didn't have my car. It was time for bed when they got home. I had called her and told her what had happened so she fed and bathed them at her house while she waited for me to get home. Sitters then were much less expensive than they are now but still the bill for childcare was getting out of hand with episodes such as these.

My car was home in time for me to go to work the following morning. Fred just drove it into the drive. His wife had followed him in their car. He felt no need to explain, justify, or apologize.

Several months later, I was on call from the hospital. I'd taken the kids to my mother's because I wanted to go out for a couple of hours with friends for pizza and beer. I could have gotten someone else, but Jocey wanted to see her grandmother. I left my car at Mother's and rode to the restaurant with one of the girls in the group. While I was at the restaurant, I got a call from the hospital: I was needed for surgery. Because I was only five minutes away from the hospital, I took a cab, expecting that the party would continue and I'd be back within an hour and a half. The operation lasted three hours. I called Mother to ask if someone could come and get me and she told me nobody was there to transport me.

Once again, I had to get home the best way I could. To my surprise, Chuckie—one of the hospital technicians with whom I worked—was still at the restaurant. She came to the hospital to get me. When I got to Mother's, there was no snow under my car and David had been asleep for hours by the looks of things. It had been snowing since noon. If he had taken the car as I had been told, there would have been snow under the car. Chuckie just looked at me and smiled; his look said, "OK, it doesn't matter."

We had briefly discussed my mother. She knew a little about the troubles I was having. Chuckie was a sweet person and would have been a good friend if I had allowed it. I didn't want a friend other than my friend Patti with whom I had grown up. I wanted no more people in my life— it was hard to manage what I had. Patti was having a rather bad time in her marriage then and I didn't have time for others' pain because I, myself, was having such a difficult time functioning.

About six months after I went to work at Marten Place Hospital I met a man who was an X-Ray technician there. A couple of weeks later we went out for an evening. My father watched the children that night. Mother was furious. She said I was disgracing Charles' memory. Of course, Charles was the man I should never have married, according to my mother, but now I was disgraceful for going out to dinner with someone from work.

As it turned out, he was wrong for having dinner with me. He was married. I knew nothing about him or his life until I arrived at work the next morning. My friend Chuckie was on my case from the moment I clocked in. She knew he was married and mentioned it when I told her what a boring time I'd had.

I waited until the female tech from X-Ray called to tell me no patients were expected for a while, and then went to the X-Ray department. The department's staff was all there. I'd warned a friend I was coming. It was lunchtime, but no one was going to miss this show. As I went into the department, I called him. In a very loud voice I told him what a boring time I'd had the night before and that I thought he was a little lower than dirt. The only reason I wasn't going to call his wife was that I didn't want to hurt her, and that if he ever spoke my name again to anyone again at work I would kick the living crap out of him. The jerk quit his job a couple of weeks later.

I never again believed anything a man told me when I first met him. Except for two, I never again dated a man who was not a professional. I made sure they had more to lose than I did if they were the type who exploited women.

I found that lawyers made good one-night stands. For most of my personal life after Charles' death, that was all I wanted. I never remarried. On the night before Charles died, I'd promised him I would not remarry. I have never regretted that promise. I came close, but it didn't happen.

For many years now, I have not used his name. After I started sleeping around, I never felt as if I should.

***

The kids and I did well when we were left alone. The problem was the advice that people volunteered. Most evenings we went somewhere, anywhere. I did anything to get away from friends and family. My kids were having a wonderful time. We went to early movies on school nights, to the beach on weekends, shopping at the malls, to visit the Zoo in Royal Oak, and on short trips when I wasn't working and the kids were out of school for the weekends. Jocey was the only one who didn't always want to go out with me. She either wanted to visit her girlfriends, her grandmother, or her cousin Jill. When my brother Louis allowed Jill to be with us, I would go after her and take her with us. We tried for a month to get to the beach. Each time I was called into the OR. When the person who was on call couldn't go in, I had to substitute. Fall was rapidly approaching, so we finally gave up and started going to the parks.

Chapter 11: Mother Again!

I'd experienced a nearly unbelievable trauma, and it had permeated every facet of my life for a very long time. Charles was no longer there to share problems and assist me. Nor were resources for individual, personal emotional help available. The local Catholic priests just were not trained to counsel those who had experienced what the kids and I had lived through. At that time, even psychiatrists could not properly treat PTSD as they can today. About all they could offer was medications. I was never a pill-taker and wasn't about to give drugs to my children.

Unable to do differently, I unfortunately placed myself and my children too close to my domineering mother, and while I worked and did what I could to make life as normal as possible for my children, the nights were filled with assorted bouts of terror. Abject loneliness became a controlling theme in my life.

While the move to Barkman Street was certainly liberating, the agony at night of not having someone with whom to discuss day's events and decide the next day's happenings was ongoing.

Enter Daniel Golden. Late in the summer of 1959, Jocey went to Long Island, New York, to visit my cousin Maizie and her family. She flew on American Airlines by herself and my cousin met her at the airport. I was to drive there a week later to pick her up. Since I had never been to Maizie's house after she'd moved to Long Island from Manhattan, Monica, the wife of my late husband's close friend Jake, was to travel with me. Jake had been trying to date me since a couple of months after Charles' death. Jake and Monica had been married almost as long as we had, but that didn't seem to deter him. He was one of the many men who wanted to "help a poor grieving widow." Jake was only the beginning of my education about...

Men!

At the last minute, Monica had to work and could not go but volunteered her brother Daniel to accompany me. I was acquainted with Danny Golden. He'd been at a few of the parties Charles and I'd attended at Monica's home. At that time, I'd never driven out of state by myself so I invited Danny to make the trip with me. The trip to NYC was uneventful for the most part. The night following our arrival, Danny and I went to some of the clubs in the city. We took the subway into Manhattan instead of driving, which was a grave mistake. The subway was filthy. I wore a white silk after-five dress and it was nearly ruined. After the subway ride, my dress was covered in flakes of soot. As soon as we arrived at the first club, I went to the woman's lounge to get help from the attendant. Those women can work miracles. In a few minutes, my dress was nearly as good as new.

Danny managed to stay sober even though I knew from other sources that he was a heavy drinker. After the weekend, Jocey, Daniel, and I returned to Michigan. During the entire trip, I never allowed him to drive my car, even though he stayed sober. According to his sister, he was a careless driver, drunk or sober.

I did not see Danny for nearly a year after the trip. My sister-in-law, Waynetta, and I went to Monica's house one evening during the summer of 1960. By now, she and my brother Fred had separated. Monica had frequent gatherings of friends at her home. These parties were usually held in the evenings.

Waynetta met someone there that night and left the party with him early. She had attended these parties with Charles and me before and knew most of the people. I didn't see her until the next day. Danny and I talked most of the time that night. He asked me for a date the next night but I declined. After the fiasco with the X-Ray technician at the hospital, I was very confused about men in general. When Charles died, I'd had very little experience with men other than male family members. I'd dated only one other boy besides Charles before we married. That date lasted the length of the movie and ice cream following the show. Steve Paone and I were both in the tenth grade at St. Charles Parochial School.

I had too many things going on in my life at that time to add a man. My life was rapidly becoming overwhelming. I had driven my car to Monica's house that night. I couldn't find Waynetta. Monica told me she had left, so I drove home alone.

At Monica's next party I arrived in a very depressed mood because the day had been a series of small disasters, both at work and at home, made worse by Mother's mouth. Mother had decided that I was the worst mother in the world and didn't hesitate to advise me of that fact. Mother had this strange perception that nobody but she could do anything right. I hadn't eaten dinner with the kids. I'd just sat at the table with them and drank coffee while they ate. I was simply too upset to eat.

I was very tired when I arrived at Monica's that night. For the first time in my life, I drank far too much. I just wanted to forget about what was happening in my life, how

I was losing control. In that state of inebriation, I was easy pickings for any man and ended up in a motel with Danny.

After midnight, we left the party together and walked the short distance to the motel. I'd driven alone to the party. I was drunk but not too drunk to know I shouldn't drive. Only family members were allowed to drive my car. I wasn't about to call home and have someone come get me. Mother would have reminded me about it until her dying day! I could have stayed at Jake's and Monica's home but for whatever reason, I must not have thought of that as a solution.

We had both drunk too much. While unusual, this time I was as drunk as everyone else at the party. Danny never took advantage of my drunkenness to have sex with me. What happened that night was as much my fault as his. We had a few motel meetings during the next few weeks—by no means was it a whirlwind courtship.

I never brought Daniel home with me or had him meet me at my house. I usually picked him up at his mother's house. Our relationship lasted about a month. When I discovered I was pregnant—I spent the next nine months vomiting with each of my pregnancies—I was greatly surprised, since the jerk (when he was sober) had told me he was sterile. When I asked him who the doctor was who'd told him he was sterile, I could not believe his answer. "I dated a girl for more than a year and she had not become pregnant," he said," so I thought I was sterile." I wanted to kill him. This man was not a teenager. He was twenty-four. How could a man that age be so naïve as to think—without medical evaluation—that he was sterile?

I was as naïve as he. From the beginning of this relationship, I should have asked him why he wore no condom or why he thought he was sterile. I knew he wasn't well informed. After I told him that I was pregnant, he told me he had discussed the matter with his family and asked me to marry him. I told him to drop dead. I've never seen him again. Not for a very long time did he see his daughter, Liza.

The day he asked me to marry him and I declined was the beginning of my "disposable" relations with men. I suppose what I was doing then in my personal life was what women are doing today. The big difference between my generation of women and today's women is that in those days, we didn't broadcast our personal lives to in graphic detail to anyone willing to listen.

The men of that generation mostly had different thoughts about women. Then, often men thought that if a woman were willing to have sex with them they must be in love with the man or she wouldn't be willing to give up her virginity. In the sixties, most women were virgins when they married, according to the nuns at St. Charles Parochial School—if they are to be believed. Only prostitutes and women like me who didn't want a commitment had sex and never looked back. Prostitutes had sex with men for money. I had sex with men because for a while I could escape.

My mother tried to force me to have an abortion, but I refused. She even went so far as to take the two checks I got from Social Security that month out of the mailbox without my knowledge, deposited them to her own checking account, and located and paid an abortionist. I should have reported her to the postal authorities but I didn't.

Flashback: Once when Charles was still living, I'd called the local police and asked them to make her bring Scotty home. I had asked her to bring him home before Charles arrived home from work. He was not in school during the summer. Mother told me she was keeping him overnight. She didn't ask—she told me her plans. We had other plans for the night. It was my night off and we were going to a drive-in show after dinner. The police called Mother, and of course, she made them believe it was all a mistake. She told them I had given her permission to keep Scotty overnight and had forgotten. Mother was going to great lengths to make my married life impossible.

Many times, I witnessed the evil of Mother's games with my brothers' wives, until one by one they each divorced my brothers. Mother had attempted control of each of her children's families. I'd have welcomed her advice if she had truly wanted to help, but all she wanted was control. Fred was married three times and was divorced each time, largely because of Mother.

David was married only once for eleven months. Mother had asked them to live with our parents until they could save money to purchase a house. David's wife Arvella took their baby and left David after a time because he wouldn't move from my parents' home and had given the money they should have saved for a new house to his mother.

When Louis returned from Korea, he married and moved away from Mother's daily interference. When Mother died in 1990, Louis had not seen her in ten years even though they lived fewer than two miles apart. His wife would often come to see Mother when I cared for her and brought gifts, but she was always alone. Joyce and Louis were married for fifty years; they died from lung cancer within six months of each other by 1999.

Another flashback: When Charles was alive, Mother had attempted to control Jason one time when he was approximately seven months of age. I was working at the hospital. Mother stopped by to see the children. It was a beautiful summer afternoon; most of the kids were outside playing in the back yard. Charles was feeding Jason before putting him to bed for a nap. The baby was cranky and didn't want to eat. Mother took the baby from his father's arms and started to put him to bed without the rest of his dinner. Charles took the baby back and called a cab for my mother. The story she told to me was unlike what had happened between the two of them. However, Mother never allowed the truth to interfere with a good story.

When I was about six weeks pregnant with Liza, I had to be admitted to Grace Hospital in Detroit. X-Rays showed that I had stones in an organ where my gall bladder should have been. For years, I'd repeatedly had kidney infections. None of my general practitioners had ordered studies to determine why. Further tests found that I had three kidneys and the extra one had stones. I stayed a month there while the doctor decided what to do. Finally, He decided to postpone the surgery until sometime in the future because the blood supply to the kidneys was not adequate to get a good tie.

Because of the position of the extra collective system, the arterial system was smaller than normal to the kidneys. After surgery or during the removal of the extra one, should I begin to bleed, I would most likely bleed to death. Years later when I had my first kidney operation to remove the stones I did hemorrhage and needed blood replacement. I still have my three kidneys: the extra collection system cannot be removed. I've had four kidney surgeries to remove stones. One of my sons and a granddaughter also have the same problem. I inherited this condition from my mother.

Chapter 12: Diabolical Plans

While I was hospitalized the first time, Mother called to tell me not to worry about my house and the kids should I die during the operation. How might you feel if a parent called while you are in the hospital to assure you that should you die, everything is in order? She'd given me permission to die, and I wasn't going to give her the satisfaction.

She and Fred had planned what they would do. She would move into my house and raise my children. I made a solemn promise to myself that day that I would not predecease her. It is one of the reasons I am still here, I suppose. I am nothing if not a survivor.

Liza Mary Bennett was born at 5:00 p.m. on June 2, 1961, at Warren Memorial Hospital, where I worked for a short period while Charles was alive. You'll note that Liza received my married name, not the name of her father, Golden. I was not proud of my conduct with Danny Golden, and I certainly wasn't going to commit the child's life to a parent such as he. She was my child alone. In Michigan, the baby takes the last name of the mother at the time of birth. She has Charles' last name, Bennett.

I'd worked with a woman at that hospital—Patricia— who was still employed in the OB/GYN department. She named the child Liza. The C-section was not done until late in the afternoon and she stayed to care for the baby that evening. I refused to identify the father, so no one notified Danny, per my orders. A month later Liza was baptized at an American Indian Catholic Church in Harbor Beach, Michigan where the kids and I were staying for a couple of months until school started and I returned to work. Scotty gave Liza the saint's name "Mary" at her baptism. Her godparents were two Indians from the Chippewa Tribe at Sault Ste. Marie, Michigan.

For the remainder of the year after her birth I stayed home with her and the other children. I didn't go back to work until she was nearly two years old. After returning to work, it became harder for me to keep up with everything I had to do. My kidney stones were bothering me again, so I quit working for the second time. Financially I was able to meet my obligations until I could get my mind to function on the all the daily tasks of living.

Before that could happen, my mother and brother Fred began to take over the house, and I wasn't happy about it. One day I came home from shopping and found I couldn't get into my own house. My key wouldn't open the doors because the dead bolt locks were in place. After I had knocked for quite a while, Fred came to the door and asked what I wanted. When I said I would like to get into *my* house he told me to go to Mother's because he had taken the smaller kids to her. He would call me when he was ready to leave. It would be in time for me to be home when the other kids got there from school. He appeared at the door wearing a woman's robe and was obviously entertaining one of his women. I went to Mother's house and returned with my children. I requested the return of the key.

A few weeks later, I had company—Monica and her children had come to visit. In walked Mother, who boldly asked, "What is *she* doing here?" referring to me, as if I were the renter and she the owner. In my own house! I was so embarrassed and humiliated. I didn't know what to say.

Mother was "checking up" on me. A nosier mother one could never have.

Monica and Mother both left in just a few minutes. I knew I couldn't continue living like this. It was hours after they both were gone and my children were in bed before I could finally sleep. By two in the morning, I was awake again, as upset as when I went to sleep only a couple of hours before. I got up, sat in the kitchen, and drank a full pot of coffee before I was finished with my plans.

The next day I called a used furniture dealer and sold all the furniture. After he looked at the furniture, he told me he could not give me what the furniture was worth. I told him to write out a check for whatever he could afford. He gave me $500. Mother—or anyone who wanted it—could have the house. I was through with it. The house had been purchased with money from Charles' insurance. I felt guilty about living there. I didn't want the house if he couldn't live there with us. I wouldn't leave the furniture for anyone. With my own money, I'd purchased every piece of it that didn't come from the TV show. If I wanted to give it away for less than a tenth of its value that was my business.

Within two days, the kids and I were in Florida. We stayed two weeks while I contemplated moving there. When I returned, I went in the other direction—to Canada—where we stayed another two weeks. I returned to Detroit and rented a house when it was time to send the children back to school.

I never returned to the house on Barkman. I had to run away or lose my mind. Dr. Julius Fink, a psychiatrist, told me that if I didn't get away from my mother, I'd go crazy. I let the house be repossessed by the bank.

Mother wanted me to keep it so we could all live together. I've never seen Mother and Fred angrier. I didn't have to tell them why—they knew. I eventually lost the war but I won that battle! The disastrous outcome of this battle was that the children and I didn't have a home of our own when we returned from our long vacation. We stayed at a motel for a few days and then I rented a house in Pontiac.

When Liza was little, I told her and the other children that Liza's father was not Charles and that her father was still alive; when and if she ever wanted to contact him, I would make it possible. I did. Years later, after Liza was discharged from the Army, she asked if I knew where her father was living. I told her I knew how to find him and would do so under one condition—she was never to tell him where I was or anything else about my life. She agreed.

I called Monica and gave Liza's phone number to her. He could call her at that number if he wanted to meet his daughter. She saw him several times over a two-year period. At first, she seemed to enjoy the visits. She told me that they went out on his boat on weekends with her husband and her two children. She said he had a nice house in the city of Lake Saint Clare, Michigan. He lived about five miles from her house. Then suddenly she stopped talking about him.

I learned from one of her sisters that he was always drunk or hung over after the first few months. Liza didn't like to have her children around him if he was always going to be drunk. Not long ago she told me that Liza has not contacted him since 1986. I knew I'd judged Danny correctly. Even as early as twenty-four, I knew he had the earmarks of a future drunk.

Liza has always been happy with her siblings. In fact, the children never refer to each other as half-sister or half-brother. They have loved each other from the day I brought her home from the hospital. The children didn't know I was expecting a baby before they saw her in the crib that day. Because of the vomiting, I'd gained little weight, and was frequently hospitalized during the pregnancy.

They were all around the crib after school that day, asking if we could keep her. The next question was about her name. I told them that she would have only a first name until she was baptized. She would be given a saint's name at that time, which would be her middle name. For several days at time they argued about who was to feed her the bottle when she was hungry. Even Shirley, as young as she was at the time, wanted her turn at feeding time. Jason liked everything about his new sister but the diapers.

I didn't have enough experience with men to make good choices in relationships. My emotional state at that time from the PTSD didn't make for good choices either. After the X-Ray technician and Danny, I didn't trust myself with men and decided not to believe any of them other than my father. I decided to play the game by their male rules. Anything men could do I would do better. "Love 'em and leave 'em" became my motto.

I would have one more child out of wedlock with a man named Rayford "Mickey" Dawson. Her name is Elizabeth Ann.

Chapter 13: Reformation

Between Danny and Elizabeth Ann's father, Mickey Dawson, I dated only once. After Mickey, it was a different story all together. I made fools out of every one of them and enjoyed every minute. I think about all the times I have put myself in harm's way and wonder how I lived to be my age. I did take protection with me on all these dates: I was never without a gun close by.

The children went to greet the *Beatles* when they landed at the airport in Detroit the night before their appearance there. We had a great time. Shirley was in kindergarten at the time. Liza and Jason were too young to be in such a large crowd. Elizabeth Ann had not yet been born. A man behind us asked me if I wanted him to hold Shirley on his shoulders. He was there with his wife and children. She had a great view of *Beatles* from atop his shoulders. The *Beatles* stayed at the Whittier Hotel in Indian Village, a very ritzy section of Detroit. The kids wanted to follow their limo to the hotel, so we had a very wild ride that night. We were not the only people following that car, so the police didn't ticket anyone. The next night we attended the show and Cathy and Mickey got their autographs. That was the highlight of her young life.

When we were alone, we had such good times. I suppose it had a lot to do with the fact that I was only twenty-five and we all enjoyed the same music and arts. Four years or so later, our family fun ended when I moved to California. I fully intended to send for the kids in fewer than six months. That never happened.

I flew to L.A. in May of 1965. Two days later, I was working for a nursing agency. I stayed there for a few weeks until I went to work at Good Samaritan Hospital, where I received benefits. Good Samaritan Hospital is where Edward Kennedy was taken after Sirhan Sirhan shot him while he was campaigning in L.A. the following year. I worked there for about six months until one of the doctors asked me to go home with his aunt who had been a patient on the floor where I was working. I cared for her until she died a few months later. I was well paid for my services and her domain was a riot.

The day my patient died, a bird flew into the open window, which was itself very strange since we were on the fourth floor of an apartment building on the ocean shore in Malibu, California. The maid said at once when she saw the bird that my patient would die that day and she did. The maid herself was strange.

While I worked there, I purchased a car. It was one of the first Mustangs. I picked the car up at the dealer's showroom on the day of the Watts riots. On the way home, the car was dented by a large rock thrown by a rioter. Two weeks later, the car was taken by someone I thought was a friend. I was not very wise in my selection of men.

I met Bob Provanco, but I don't recall where. It wasn't at a bar because I was never a bar hopper. In my life, I have been in a bar fewer than two dozen times at most. I cannot tolerate drunks. The relationship with Bob lasted about two weeks when he came to the hospital one afternoon to borrow my new car. He was to be back in time to get me after my shift. He never showed up. When my car had not been returned by the next morning, I called the police. My car was found three days later in *Harrod's* parking lot in Reno, Nevada. I took off from work for the next two days and flew that night to Reno to get the car. The doors were locked. The police did not have the keys and neither did Bob. He was in jail for parole violation. He had never mentioned that.

The relationship would not have lasted much longer anyway for a couple of reasons. The man ruined a very good steak that I had cooked for him one evening. Who would put catsup on a prime rib? I could not believe he was such a moron!

The car was not damaged so I just forgot about him. That was easy to do. Getting a key made to move the car was a little more difficult.

Mickey was a friend (read "drinking buddy") of Bob. I later discovered that they belong to the same AA club. He came to my apartment one afternoon looking for Bob. I told him Bob was in jail for stealing my car and for parole violations. I was trying to affix the new plate to my car and Mickey volunteered to do it for me. Later when I got home from work, he stopped by my apartment again. It was nearly midnight and I was tired. I told him if he was an early bird, I generally ate breakfast at a nearby coffee shop about eight. When he showed up that morning, I should have realized he was not employed. Day workers are usually at work by then. In fact, he was on his way to an AA meeting. I did not find out about his drinking until sometime later.

After several dates, a short trip across the border to Mexico, and some time spent discussing my children and my plans to have them with me before much longer, Mickey and I moved in together. We decided to pool our money so the kids could come out within a few weeks. I found a house I liked in Covina, a twenty-minute drive from LA and the hospital where I worked. He paid the deposit and the first month's rent. I still did not know where he worked, but I thought it must be a substantial. He always seemed to have money.

I was so engrossed in my plans to have the children with me that I stupidly overlooked many warnings until it was too late. All I could think about was being a family again. I had promised Charles the night before he died that I would never marry again and here I was planning a wedding. I would live with Mickey until I had the children home with me and bought a house, and then we would go our separate ways. My thought processes were beginning to be very messed up. I knew right from wrong; I just didn't care anymore. If I had the kids back with me and away from Mother and Fred, right and wrong was a concern only for others.

It is logical to ask why it would be necessary for me to marry. I don't know. Even though I had every intention to use Mickey, accumulate my family and leave, the appearance of permanence had to be carried out to block any blowback from my mother.

I'd lost all I was going to lose in this lifetime. The kids had lost their father and his love for them. God did not care, nobody else cared, and I had to do whatever I could to survive in this horrible world! I could not die. I was as healthy as the proverbial horse. I could not kill myself; I'd tried that but could not leave the kids alone.

There was nothing else to do, as I saw it. I would get the kids, go to nursing school, buy a house, and live as happily as possible. Nothing or no one would stop me. I'd use people as they had used me and the Devil may care. The hate for men that was building within me was almost uncontrollable. If I'd been a man, I might have ended up a serial killer.

A few weeks before the Christmas holidays, we made plans to drive to Michigan and get the kids. All I could think about was the trip. I'd become obsessed with my plans. It was all I thought about day and night. As I look back now, I realize how few of those plans included Mickey. My mind was developing a true skill of not thinking about too far into the future. Get through this day first and then deal with tomorrow's woes when they occur. "Never doubt," I told myself, "that tomorrow will have more than its share of woes."

The morning we were to leave for Michigan finally arrived. I had taken time off from work. Just before we were to leave, a young man I'd never seen before arrived at the house. He and Mickey left for a short time. I was visibly upset. It seemed as if they were gone for hours but, it was much less. When they returned, Mickey couldn't leave quick enough. It was the first time I'd seen him drunk. Within a short time, he was passed out on the front seat of my car. My anger at the drunk in my car went off all known charts. This anger confirmed my resolve to dump this idiot as soon as financially possible.

I did the driving to Michigan but the drunk gave the route to me. Without my questioning, he directed us to Dallas, Texas. It was sometime later that I learned why. Prior to our departure, the worthless idiot had robbed a bank that morning with the young man who had showed up at the house before we left for the trip. It was a good thing I did not find out about the robbery until he was already in jail. I would have buried that bastard in the desert before we ever reached the Mississippi River. After all, the man who had caused my husband's death got away with it, didn't he? That man barely knew Charles. This drunk was helping me to destroy any possibility of happiness with my children. From that point on, I loathed him and began to think of ways to assist his demise.

The trip became a disaster. I was able to spend a few days with the children away from my family but at the end of the time with them, Mickey told me he was out of money. I had only enough to get the two of us back to California, and despite his promises, Mickey refused to take the children along.

I cannot express in words the way I felt—language is inadequate and I was running out of strength to protest. I was returning to Covina without the only people besides my father that I cared about. On the trip back, I vowed that I would still get the kids and that Mickey would pay for what he had just done to the kids and me.

A few weeks after we returned, I found I was pregnant. What was I going to do now? I could not kill the father of my child even though he deserved to die, in my mind. What would I tell the child when it was an adult? "I killed him because he was a stupid bastard but I love you and you are a beautiful person?" If it hadn't been for my work, I think I would have gone crazy.

One afternoon I arrived home from work to find Mickey in the garage with the neighbor from next door. He suggested that he had a strong interest in the man. Mickey was even a poor liar. Did he not have any redeeming qualities? He wasn't a good lover. That didn't bother me because I wasn't in this relationship for romance. Since I was the only one working full time, I continued to work until the night before I went into the hospital.

I had been hospitalized twice with kidney problems since becoming pregnant this time. The C-Section was scheduled for the month of September near the end of the month. On August 1, I staggered next door (to the man who was in the garage with Mickey) for help. I was in no condition to drive to Good Samaritan Hospital and Mickey, unbelievably, was working for a change. The wife of Mickey's friend drove me to the hospital.

When admitted, I was put into a private room in the labor and delivery room section. The nurse got orders from the attending OB/GYN doctor. At once, there was an IV hung and I was wrapped in heated bath blankets because I was nearly in shock. My urologist was summoned and a cardiologist was asked to consult. I was having horrible dreams, which the physicians blamed on my condition but I knew that was not the cause. I never discussed the dreams or the screaming in my sleep with any of the people who cared for me. It had nothing to do with my kidneys and I at this time did not want to talk about my life.

On August 10, three physicians gathered at the foot of my bed to tell me that they had decided to operate that morning. It was the only way they could keep me alive and get a viable baby. The little girl born a couple of hours later was six weeks' premature. Her weight was three pounds and eleven ounces.

I went back to work when she was four weeks old because I needed money to pay my car payment and the rent. I would not be able to save for the kids' trip and support Mickey and a four-bedroom house. An ultimatum was forming. He had either to go or start bringing home money regularly.

I had tolerated all the part-time work and the occasional withdrawal from my bank account I was going accept from Mickey. There was also some strong evidence that he was making some bank withdrawals of money that wasn't his to take.

When Elizabeth Ann was born, Cathy sent a Catholic medal to me that she'd received from one of the nuns. It depicted the newly canonized saint Sister Elizabeth Ann Seton. St. Elizabeth was our country's first Saint. "Lizard Ann" had not been named when I received the medal in the mail. I thought it would please Cathy if I named the baby after the new saint. Today Elizabeth Ann now is a beautiful woman with an adult daughter, Savannah, whom she raised by herself. Elizabeth divorced when Savannah was fourteen months old. Years later, when Cathy was on a trip to Jamaica with her graduating class, she mailed a post card to Elizabeth Ann. The picture on the card was of a large lizard. So I started calling her "Lizard Ann." She hates this nickname; today I am the only person who occasionally calls her by that name.

Mickey was happy just to stay home with the baby and care for her while I worked. He must have thought I was crazy or that I was so much in love with him that I would do anything to keep him. He was wrong on both counts. Little did he know how much I hated him and what I had planned for his future. If my plan worked, Mickey would soon make his last bank "withdrawal."

On the day I made this decision, the baby was about six weeks old. I did not go into work that day so I would not be arriving home after midnight and find the fool sleeping. After dinner, and when I had put the baby into bed, I sat down in the kitchen and told the SOB that his gravy train had left the station without him. I would no longer support him. I gave him one week to get his act together or he was to pack his bags and leave.

He must have thought I was joking. During the next few days, he never left the house. When I was sure he was making no effort to find work, I called in sick and stayed home again. The next morning I woke him about six a.m. While he was having his coffee, I walked over to him and told him that if he weren't going to work he had better successfully rob his next bank or I would turn him into the police for the others I knew about. I also told him that I planned to be at my mother's house in Michigan within the next two weeks, packing the kids' things for the trip back to California. He just sat there speechless. When he did speak he angrily yelled, "If you say anything to anyone about me I will tell the authorities you planned and forced me to commit them."

Why he never told me then that he hadn't robbed any banks since he'd been released from jail, I don't know. Perhaps he was beginning to fear what I might do. I looked at him, not changing my facial expression one bit, and told him to go ahead if he thought the police would believe him since he had spent eighteen years for bank robbery before he ever met me.

He was not aware until that moment that I had checked on his past. His face never showed fear—just shock. I never allowed him to know how much that threat worried me, and rightly so. He stormed out of the house after calling someone. He waited in the garage for the person to appear. I recognized the man who had been with him the morning we went to Michigan during the winter holidays.

Chapter 14: Best of Detentions

Three days later, Mickey came home with theatrical makeup and false hair. He was up late that night getting everything ready for the following morning. I drove him to a lot in downtown LA to rent a car. That was my big mistake! That one act sent me to prison for nearly three years.

I have wished numerous times since that day I'd never driven him anywhere that morning. If I had only allowed him to take my car I could have said I didn't know what he was planning to do because he'd taken the car without my permission and I would have been believed. One of the Federal officers later told me I would have gotten away with it. He said under the circumstances, he would not charge me if he had control over the situation, but sadly he didn't. I was charged with aiding and abetting an armed bank robbery.

That charge handed Mother my kids on a silver platter. It was a blessing for Mickey that he was not allowed out on bond, as was I. I would have killed the bastard if I could have gotten my hands on him. He couldn't do anything right. He was worthless as far as I was concerned. In my lifetime I have hated two men, the man who killed Charles with his greed and the worthless Mickey. In my mind, he didn't deserve to live after ruining the lives of my children.

I fully accepted my horrible mistake in becoming involved with Mickey. I had wanted his financial help to get my children from Michigan to California. When we met, I thought he was working and would help me save money for the move. I had nothing to do with Charles' death. I did not have a reason to hate myself as I hated Mickey for betraying me. I hated him with all my heart.

I hired an attorney and Mickey had a public defender, along with the young man whom he had duped. The kid was an alcoholic. Mickey told this kid he had robbed banks since he was a teen. The kid believed Mickey but I will never understand why I believed him. I suppose I was suffering from tunnel vision. I wanted one thing and one thing only—my children in California with me. I couldn't see any other way. I simply couldn't return to Michigan. I could not stand to live one more day there. If I had gone home, I truly believe I would have taken the children's lives and mine. I suppose prison saved my physical life while messing with my already-troubled mind. I deserved my sentence but the children didn't deserve what happened to them.

Mickey had been borrowing money from different people. One of them was the young man who went to jail with him for the bank robbery. I don't recall his name; he must have been about twenty-two. I don't know where they met. I did not know him or anything about him. If I ever knew his name, I've forgotten it. He never made bond. After his trial, I never saw him again. Since he was under twenty-five, he received a Youth Act Sentence that prohibited him from spending more than seven years in prison, as opposed to Mickey's twenty years. Mickey served eighteen years in prison, plus five years extra for the letter he sent to me before he was released (see below).

At one point following Mickey's release, Elizabeth Ann asked if I could find him because she wanted to write to him. She was curious. I didn't know where he lived but I knew how to find him. He would be in the Bureau of Prison files because I was almost certain he was on parole. I had answered his letters for a while after he went to prison and then I stopped. The letters were mostly about the baby. She was the only thing we had in common.

In 1970, about a year after I was released and Elizabeth Ann and I had returned to Detroit, a letter came from Mickey. He was still in prison. I had no idea how he obtained my address or how he knew I was living in Detroit. The return address was McNeil Island Federal Correctional Institute (Washington State) but it was postmarked LA. Obviously, he had arranged for a departing inmate to post the letter. He wanted no censorship.

When I open the letter and started to read, I panicked. He was telling me that he would have someone pick up my daughter and keep her until he was released if I didn't start writing to him. I never finished reading the letter.

At once, I phoned the prison and asked to speak with the chaplain. He wasn't there but his aide said he would give him my message as soon as he arrived. That evening after I was home from work the chaplain called. There is a three-hour difference between Washington State and Detroit, Michigan. He had been trying all day to get in touch with me. I read the letter to him. He said he would handle it at once.

Early the following morning two agents from the FBI were at my door. They were there for most of the morning talking to me. Both men were very concerned for our safety. I was asked if it was possible for me to move to another house. That would not be a problem, I told them, because I had been looking at houses to buy. My cousin's former sister-in-law was in real estate. I had almost decided on a house to buy before the letter had arrived.

What I had not planned to do was to change my name but the agents wanted me to do just that, to make it a little harder to find me. I now had two people wanting to get even with me—the person who had posted the letter for Mickey when he was caught and Mickey, who received more time for sending the letter. I told them I would change my name before I purchased a new house hoping that would make finding us a little more difficult. This was the beginning of a series of name changes necessitated by one pinch after another.

When this happened with the letter, Elizabeth Ann was only three or so. A friend of mine, Ron Lyle, said I could use his last name if I wanted. When Elizabeth Ann was registered in school a few years later, she was already using the name Lyle. When they left, one of the agents took the letter as evidence. Mickey would receive another charge. The letter had not been sent from the prison but was illegally taken out by a visitor. That is a felony. Mickey was given five more years. I never heard if the person who had mailed the letter was caught.

Years later, when I told Elizabeth Ann where she could write to her father, I also told her what he had threatened to do many years before. I asked her to be very careful about writing to him and never to meet him by herself. She later showed a picture of her dad to me. It nearly made me ill to see his face again. She also gave a letter to me he had sent in the same envelope as hers. I read it while she stood there. He said he thought it was about time we got married. I told her to tell her father if he ever tried to contact me again, I would call the FBI.

She wrote to him a few times before she also gave up on him. I don't know what he wrote to her after the first letter but it must have been nothing she cared to hear because the pen pal relationship lasted less than a month. She never speaks of him.

When I spoke with Mickey's parole officer, the man was shocked. Mickey had told him that the baby and I had been killed in an auto accident shortly after I had been released from prison. He just couldn't believe any woman would leave him, I suppose. After I finished telling the parole officer I was trying to contact Mickey only because his daughter had asked, the officer told me to write a letter stating that I wanted nothing to do with him.

The parole officer made a copy of the letter and gave it to Mickey. The original letter from me he put into Mickey's file. Two people in my lifetime have told others of my so-called death: my mother and Mickey. I'm still around and they are both deceased.

I was given four years but served only two years and a few months in prison. While I was in prison, I was assigned to work in the sewing room, since I knew how to sew. I enjoyed the work. We made items that were purchased by *Sears* and sold in their retail stores. Then, American jobs were not outsourced to other countries. We also made both uniforms and street clothes for the prison population. As a teenager, I learned to do commercial sewing from a neighbor who made garments for a factory in Detroit.

I was in prison when I had serious kidney complications, requiring surgery. It was done at the prison hospital. The operation nearly killed me. I hemorrhaged; the doctor used blood from one of the inmates with my blood type. Two weeks later, I learned I had Hepatitis-B.

When I wasn't working, I spent my spare time reading and taking classes offered by the local college. The other women loved that I wasn't a television watcher. After dinner and headcount each night, a different woman had control of the shows seen by all in their housing unit. I had many favors done for me by those who wanted my night each time it came around. I was too busy studying. I went to classes during part of the day. I worked from noon until four each day. The instructor was qualified to teach some college classes. I did college biology (just class not lab), Mathematics, and English History. These classes were all accredited because the instructor also taught at the local community college.

I was allowed to leave prison before my sentence was finished. I had had no problems while there. I was one of only three people picked to take part in a new work release program California was instituting. Work release had not been tried in California before 1969. The three of us had no problem getting work.

Two days after I was in LA, I was working at Blue Cross, where I reviewed medical charges for payment. Alcohol or drug abuse had never been a problem in my life and I had a good work record. The woman who interviewed me for the position had to be told that I was on work release. That didn't seem to bother her because of my work record. The interviewer had me fill out a second application, which she put into the employee's file. The first application I filled out she put into her desk drawer. She told me if I had any trouble she would use the first application to fire me and she would use the second for any promotion.

The first night I was at the halfway house, one of the female guards from the prison was on duty. I was teasing her about getting work release along with me. She worked nights in my building and was about my age, thirty-five.

One night we were talking about things in general when she stopped talking in mid-sentence and told me she was glad my eyes no longer glared with hatred as they did when we first met. She said that she was frightened of me when I was admitted to her unit.

I felt the same. *Inside,* I felt as if I would need a stepladder to get out of the ditch I was in. I reflected the situations where I found myself. I did not feel emotions as I once did. If people around me looked somber, I was somber. If they were happy, I acted as if I also was happy. As the song says: Sunrise Sunset Sunrise Sunset, quickly flow the years. I was a chameleon.

While I was away, Jocey became pregnant and married (in that order. The apple doesn't fall far from the tree). She gave birth to a little girl. She had married and given birth and I hadn't been there for her either time. She was only sixteen. How much she must have hated me after I returned to California without them when I had come to get them with Mickey! I've always loved my children and my father dearly but even that love had dimmed. Over the years, that intense love has returned and matured.

Many times, I had almost given up on ever having a happy future as I slowly healed myself, a process that is still ongoing. Having my children little again and starting over with Charles and them would make the nightmares go away completely but no one can go back in time. Over the years, I've coped as well as I can. I've accepted that I will never be the person I once was. I still have the night sweats and horrible dreams at times. I've known I had PTSD since I was twenty-five, but no one understood my problem then.

Elizabeth and I returned to Detroit on May 29, 1969. I had been at the halfway house since January of that year.

Elizabeth Ann spent the last few nights at the house with me before we left LA. I had quit working and we played around and shopped for her. I didn't want to take anything back with us that had been hers while I was *inside*. My attorney, Aaron Shilling, had saved all my clothes and returned them to me the day after I was at the halfway house, along with a bottle of "My Sin" perfume. He knew it was my favorite.

Aaron had visited me many times while I was in jail. He was a sweet person, one of the few people I would have trusted with my life. I did in a way since he was my attorney! I was charged with a crime that could have gotten me fifteen years. Aaron managed to get the judge to allow me to delay turning myself in for a month after I was sentenced so I could return to Michigan to see my children. Rarely is such a request allowed since I would be traveling to another state. I stayed for a week with them. Aaron later told me the reason the judge was so understanding was because my mother had called him to ask him to give me the maximum time.

The hatred from what had happened to me when Charles was killed and the children injured on Christmas morning has ruined my life and the lives of those whom I loved and who loved me. My father was a very private person but I know he also suffered every day I was in prison. Had I known how to forgive my mother, that hatred might have been lessened.

Aaron proved, over time, to be worthy of my trust. (He died in Japan a few years ago while defending an American soldier.) I picked Elizabeth up from the home of the woman who had cared for her while I was in prison. I paid for Elizabeth's care myself. Aaron had watched over Elizabeth while she was in that home, visiting unannounced, so he would know that her good care had continuity.

Back in Michigan, sometime around June of 2000, I met a man who lived down the street from me. His wife attended the same church as I. One day as we talked over tea, I discovered he knew my brother David. They had both worked for Lacy Trucking Company in Detroit and had gone to many bars together. David was the only alcoholic in the family.

Lyle's wife died a few months later. A few weeks after the funeral he asked me to start driving for him. He was a diabetic and had lost most of his ability to see. Lyle told me that during the last couple of years before his wife died, she had been his eyes when he drove. She would tell him when the traffic lights were going to change, when to stop for stop signs, when a car was coming too close. Now that she was gone, he had no one to be his co-pilot.

For the next eighteen months, I drove him whenever he left the house. We drove to visit his son in Indiana and a few months before he died, I drove him to his Army reunion in Traverse City, Michigan. We had a great time together. He was like the big brother I did not have. He insisted on paying me the wage I would have received from someone else. This was during one of the times I had retired. I made a deal with him—he would save the money until I asked for it.

Early in 2001, I told him I wanted the money to start a women's clothing store. He wrote out a check for nearly fourteen thousand dollars. I named the store C. H. Bennett Mercantile after my husband. Only a couple of weeks before Lyle's death he gave me another large sum of money. His daughter was visiting; it was summer and she was not working. She is a school councilor somewhere in the middle of Michigan. I asked her to come and stay with him until he died. I knew it would not be long before that happened. His kidneys were rapidly failing. He was down to eight percent function and had a shunt implanted in his forearm to facilitate dialysis. She refused. I told her he would mostly likely die alone in the house. That didn't seem to upset her and he did indeed die alone while I was at the store. I went to his house after closing the store as always and found him dead on the bathroom floor. No one should die alone. He must have broken his neck when he fell off the toilet and hit the bathtub.

Now, here I am. What is the sum? Sometimes I think about all the times I have put myself in harm's way and wonder how I've lived to be my age. Psychiatrists will claim that I was living a death wish; maybe I was. I claim that each affair was a cry of desperation, and I present as evidence the fact that the nightmares and screams continued even today although they are less frequent.

Chapter 15: Retrospective

At this point, the narrative of Denise Bennett, as she presented it, ceases. In the simplest of explanations, Denise, by whatever name she currently uses, disappeared.

It could be that the store she began took a nosedive. Retail activities weren't doing all that well in the early years of the twenty-first century. Judging from the amount of money she spent when I knew her, there was no large bankroll behind her, though there was one issue that would leave me to wonder if she'd found a way to "play" the system once again.

When we began to work on her memoir, she lived at a small two-bedroom apartment not far from my house. She was working part time for the Diocese of Tucson and maintaining a cat-fostering activity for a local cat rescue organization.

For a period of about six weeks, she bombarded me with information. I filled several notebooks from our interviews. My wife and I often visited. Her information was so detailed, intertwined, and involved, that eventually I simply provided a computer for her use. I then took her ramblings and random thoughts and put them into the presentation you have been reading. We spent hours clarifying, reorganizing, rewriting, "diggin' up bones," even to the point where things were difficult for her to discuss. Based on that information gathering, and based on the observations that I made, I complete this screed with a set of what I hope are reasonable assumptions.

If this is entirely true, and I have no reason to assume that it is not, it should be obvious at this point that given the opportunity, Denise would have wished to become paint on the wall. While I could obtain a copy of the *Detroit Free Press* for Christmas Day, 1958, it involved taking out a subscription to the newspaper. I saw little point in doing so. However, I did see an incident report from the Detroit Fire Department, the contents of which are detailed in this book.

Denise had lost her husband. She'd lost her home. She'd nearly lost her physical life. Her emotional life had taken a serious beating. Her family of origin had suffered loss. She suffered loss from serious injuries and deaths of some of her children.

It is apparent from what has been presented that there was a love/hate relationship between her and her mother. Her mother opposed her original marriage (she couldn't do anything about the original pregnancy) and apparently attempted to control all aspects of her life thereafter. Denise was condemned or commended by her actions but not by her mother, whose entire focus was apparently the former. Her father didn't seem to behave that way, but from her telling of the story, her father was easily cowed. Not being privy to that relationship, I cannot comment directly upon it, except to say that from an observational standpoint, Denise's actions support the premises she has offered.

Further, I should point out, that in the previous chapter, the last of her offering, she acknowledges responsibility for the hatred that destroyed her entire family.

In 1969, following her release from prison, Denise returned to Detroit, with her youngest, intent on picking up the earlier pieces of her family and her life. By this time, of course, her older children either had attained or were approaching adulthood. Some had married; some had divorced. Her own siblings had either died or, in one case, been murdered.

For the next four years, her life was nothing as it had been. She still had to contend with her mother. Her father was gone. Finding employment wasn't easy. She had one major form of financial support—survivor benefits from Charles' Social Security. For that, she needed to operate under her original married name. That becomes important to this story. I'll come back to that. As a part of this scheme, Denise entered a change of address in care of her friend Patti. Patti would arrange the forwarding of the money from hereon.

She learned how easy it was to obtain official identification with a new name. A certificate form from a stationery store with some fancy calligraphy inscribed on it became the basis to apply for accounts and drivers' licenses. As an example: when she was imprisoned, she was living with, but was not married to, Mickey. When she knew Mickey, he was using the surname "Lappan." She had the appropriate identification documents. Thus, she became a convict named "Lappan," and nobody thought otherwise. She would learn that he was listed on his prison records as "Dawson."

She adopted Mickey's last name, though she was never married to him. She adopted an employer's name (Lyle) when she cared for the man's indigent wife, prior to her death. It didn't take long before she became more than one person officially. As I said before, I really do not know if any name contained herein is valid. She assured me they were not.

There are no doubt instances of transference, where the emotion invested in a child is transferred to another person or, as is the case here, to an animal... a kitten. Acquiring a kitten is a custom for many. I do not know how or when, but in her Michigan travels, she encountered a cat "no-kill" operation and agreed, for a fee, to "foster" a small number of kittens. It wasn't much, but it provided enough income to feed them and they, in turn, provided companionship and substitution for progeny long departed from the nest.

Kittens that are not spayed or neutered eventually become cats that produce more kittens. Those kittens did not arrive from the shelter and whose room and board Denise now had to provide by herself.

Then, there was Mother. Mother was not a cat lover. Mother made Denise's life miserable vis-a-vis the animals, especially as the number climbed. As the saga had begun, she was living in one of Mother's apartments, and Mother disliked the animals she kept.

In 1998, she became eligible for her own Social Security payment. Now, however, she was a different person with her natal SSN, and apparently, she drew benefits directly under her new name and a number that, I suspect, belonged to someone else. Eventually, even Elizabeth Ann departed, married, and as suddenly as Denise had begun her life with family, the familial situation ended. I do not know why, but I did learn that Denise was estranged from Elizabeth Ann.

Things wouldn't loosen for her personally until she, herself, began to draw Social Security. That's important also, as this Social Security check arrived in one of the assumed names.

Sometime in the early months of 2005, Denise packed the absolute minimum of her personal affairs, arranged a ride to a U-Haul outlet seventy-five miles away from Detroit, rented a small box truck, and after dark returned to her home. It was to be a twenty-four-hour rental.

She moved her boxes and luggage into the bed of the truck. She added to the load several trays of cat kibble and a handful of litter boxes, which she filled. Then, one by one, she place something more than sixty kittens inside the box truck, left the key to the house on the sideboard, closed the apartment, and headed south.

Her family had its roots in Detroit. She was married and had her first six children in Detroit. Now everything was gone and there was little point to continue to stay in Mother's house and endure grief for the remainder of her mother's life. However, where to go?

She has stated she was a trained nurse. She states that she was trained at Johns Hopkins, which, of course, is in Baltimore, Maryland. I can find no record and obtained no narrative about her being in Baltimore, so she may have received training in a California program so sponsored, around the time she was using the name under which she had been imprisoned. Licensing of nurses, however, is a function of the state of employment and a Michigan license, particularly one that was issued under another name, is hardly transferable to another state. That would block her from obtaining nursing employment in Arizona, where she ended up.

One thing for certain—Detroit is cold in the winter. If you're going anywhere, it's somewhere warm. In February and March, Routes 80 and 90 had just too many mountains, and those mountains had snow and ice. That left Route 66 out of Chicago, headed south and then west.

She drove and pulled into rest areas to sleep, preferably isolated areas where the sounds of the cats couldn't be detected. She passed trays of food through the door to the cats but didn't remove the litter boxes until after dark.

While the cats were fed and the litter boxes were dumped, the cats needed moisture, and she added some to the kibble. Otherwise, it wasn't available. The further south she drove, the hotter it became inside the box of the U-Haul. During the hottest part of the day, she found shade and water for the animals, and then drove at night.

Along the way, she was careful to park away from other activity in the rest or refueling actions she took. Anyone walking close to the truck could hear the cats within.

It was about one in the morning near Santa Fe, the capital of New Mexico, that a State Trooper pulled the U-Haul truck over for a malfunctioning taillight. When the U-Haul box was checked for contraband and the cats were discovered, it was learned that two of the animals had died. Denise was arrested on the spot. The animals were confiscated and taken by a local rescue organization. The truck was impounded, and Denise was arrested and put in the Santa Fe County jail.

At her bail hearing the following morning, she was released on her own recognizance and directed to return in a week for trial. She jumped bail and caught a Greyhound bus headed west on Interstate 10. Tucson, Arizona, was the next major bus stop.

Later that day, officials in Santa Fe learned that U-Haul in Michigan had reported the truck as stolen. By now, Denise had melted into the countryside.

She would have preferred to go to Los Angeles, but she recognized that she had no current connections there and literally could not afford lodging should she make it there. Similarly, it was important to get out of New Mexico.

The first thing Denise did when she arrived in Tucson was to locate a place she could afford to live. She had enough money to pay a deposit and first month's rent, and enough of a silver tongue to get the rental agent to accept that she needed to arrange to have her bank account transferred to Tucson.

The next thing she did was to take the yellow pages,[15] see what banks were within walking distance of her apartment.

She began to scout them to see which would accept an account transfer on a regular basis from a bank in Detroit. Thus, when Denise's widow benefits—those that arrived in her original married name—arrived at Patti's, Patti would deposit them in the bank in Detroit and then Denise would go into the bank in Tucson and arrange a transfer. I went with her three times when she made these arrangements, not fully understanding why it was necessary. I frankly wonder why the bank itself didn't question this arrangement. This was why, later, when she dropped out of sight, the local bank could tell me they had no account for the person whose name I had provided.

---

[15]   For the Millennial reader, the "Yellow Pages" was a printed telephone book containing contact numbers of local businesses.

Now she needed work. She couldn't take up nursing and she didn't have the licenses Arizona required to provide care-giving services. Here was an example of how she entrapped herself. Her nursing credentials were in a different name.

She then took the one connection she could legitimately exploit—the Catholic Church. She found the Tucson Diocesan Office, figured out what combination of buses and walking was necessary to reach their offices, and volunteered to work. That put her in place when a few weeks later, a paid part-time position became available. Weeks after she disappeared, I approached that office to locate her, only to learn that "no such person has ever worked here" and "we have no record of her attending church."

She arrived in Tucson carrying only a suitcase. The apartment was unfurnished. One of the characteristics of Tucson is the plethora of places where you can rent furniture. There are several reasons "rent to own" organizations can flourish there. First, it's the location of a major university. Next, it's a major destination for people called "snowbirds," people who come for the winter, stay three months, and leave; some rent apartments year-round merely to have a place available to come. Finally, there is a large military presence there. Temporary housing requires furniture to function.

There are many, many apartments with refrigerators and stoves, furnaces, and sometimes air conditioners. All of them need beds, dressers, sofas, overstuffed chairs, dinette sets, and televisions added to become functionally useful.

Her first rentals-to-own were a bed, a two-chair kitchen table, and a television set. Over time, living room furniture, dressers, and red-colored matching kitchen appliances were added. Since I often conveyed her in my car, the rental agency was a frequent stop, while she made regular payments. As things became wholly hers, she'd upgrade them. She regularly upgraded her television, though she never obtained Internet service while I knew her. Later, when I was looking for her, I visited that rental agency, only to be told "no such person has an account here."

Additional support was available. Once again, she became a cat "foster-mother." My recollection was that she had about a dozen cats then. I arranged to have the back porch enclosed with chicken wire to allow her to put them "outdoors." It couldn't have produced much income, but it did produce some. Occasionally, she would "sit" with my wife, who had a form of dementia, if it were necessary for me to go to a meeting or shopping alone. If she had other sources, I do not know them.

We worked together on this book many months. In the late months of 2008, my wife had a heart attack. She was hospitalized, operated upon, spent time in rehab, and was re-hospitalized. She died early in January 2009. For the next seven months, I worked to prepare our home for sale and to prepare vehicles for the trip back to New England, my origins. To relieve Denise's debt for furniture, I donated a bedroom set, which she put in storage. When it appeared that my arrangements would find their way to order, I again approached Denise's apartment to continue our work, only to discover that she had moved, and, of course, nobody knew where.

Ultimately, I married again, and in 2014, my new wife and I visited Tucson. Again, I attempted contact, but couldn't locate her. I never again heard from her. Whether she ever finished her narration, either to the manuscript or to herself, I do not know. Since she was a frail woman with ongoing maladies, she may not have survived. If she did, she would be 89 years of age. If she did and finds this book, I hope she is satisfied with the work I've done.

She literally up and moved to another location without leaving a forwarding address, not even for the forwarding of her mail. She did contact me once, told me she was "caring for an elderly person," and promised to maintain contact. I finally located her and traced her to another residence and, when I sent someone to see her (by that time I had left Arizona), she had left again, no forwarding address. Moreover, it would appear, she had changed her name once again.